KAREN BROWN'S
Austria
Charming Inns & Itineraries

Written by

CLARE BROWN

Illustrations by Barbara Tapp

Cover Painting by Jann Pollard

Travel Press
Karen Brown's Country Inn Series

Karen Brown Titles

Austria: Charming Inns & Itineraries

California: Charming Inns & Itineraries

England: Charming Bed & Breakfasts

England, Wales & Scotland: Charming Hotels & Itineraries

France: Charming Bed & Breakfasts

France: Charming Inns & Itineraries

Germany: Charming Inns & Itineraries

Ireland: Charming Inns & Itineraries

Italy: Charming Bed & Breakfasts

Italy: Charming Inns & Itineraries

Spain: Charming Inns & Itineraries

Switzerland: Charming Inns & Itineraries

Karen Brown's Guides
Post Office Box 70
San Mateo, California 94401, USA
Tel: (415) 342-9117 Fax: (415) 342-9153
e-mail: karen@karenbrown.com

Dear Friends:

Thank you for your many letters. They help to keep us current on the over 1,600 properties in our guides. Although we personally inspect (without exception) every accommodation we recommend, places change from one visit to the next. Sometimes they improve dramatically. Sometimes they go downhill. With this in mind, we eagerly read what you, our "inspectors on the road," have to say about your personal experiences. We often receive mixed reviews—some of you rave about a property, while others have complaints. When this happens, we weigh all comments and try to make a balanced judgment—and target the property for another inspection.

Thanks too for the many spectacular discoveries you have shared with us. Many of the finest places in our guides are those you have found. Please drop us a line when you come across a real "winner." Tell us why you think it's special and if possible include a photo or a brochure.

We value all your fine letters. Please keep them coming.

Warm personal regards,

Karen   Clare   June

Editors: Clare Brown, Karen Brown, June Brown, Iris Sandilands
Technical support: William H. Brown III; Aide-de-camp: William H. Brown
Illustrations: Barbara Tapp; Cover painting: Jann Pollard; Cover design: Tara Brassil
Maps: Susanne Lau Alloway—Greenleaf Design & Graphics; Cover photo: William H. Brown
Written in cooperation with Carlson Wagonlit/Town & Country Travel, San Mateo, CA 94401, USA
Distributed USA & Canada: The Globe Pequot Press, Box 833, Old Saybrook, CT 06475, USA
Tel: (860) 395-0440, fax: (860) 395-0312
Distributed Australia & New Zealand: Little Hills Press Pty. Ltd., 1st Floor, Regent House
37-43 Alexander Street, Crows Nest NSW 2065, Australia, tel: (02) 437-6995, fax: (02) 438-5762
Distributed U.K. & Europe: Hi Marketing, 38 Carver Road, London SE24 9LT, England
Tel: (0171) 738-7751, fax: (0171) 274-9160
A catalog record for this book is available from the British Library

Library of Congress Cataloging-in-Publication Data

Brown, Clare
      Karen Brown's Austria : charming inns & itineraries / written by
  Clare Brown ; illustrations by Barbara Tapp ; cover painting by Jann
  Pollard. — 4th ed.
            p. cm.
      Originally published: Austrian country inns & castles. c 1986
      Includes index.
    ISBN 0-930328-41-8 (pbk.)
    1. Hotels--Austria--Guidebooks. 2. Austria--Guidebooks.
  I. Brown, Clare. Austrian country inns & castles. II. Title.
  III. Title: Austrian country inns & itineraries
TX907.5.A8B76 1997
    647.94436' 01--dc20   96–21925
                                                              CIP

Dedicated with Love
to
Alexandra and Richard
Emily, Christopher, and William
and Little Clare

Check out Karen Brown's Web Site at
http://www.karenbrown.com

With the click of a button you can:

Research accommodations

Select hotels by region and review color photos and information on individual properties—an excellent way to visualize and compare your choices

Make on-line reservations

Make on-line reservations at a selection of our recommended properties, as well as at other hotels around the world

Review itineraries

Investigate recommended countryside itineraries and personalized countryside mini-tours designed by Karen Brown

Connect to Karen Brown Travel Services

Just fill out our web page form or send an e-mail to Karen Brown Travel Services to book a mini-tour or to make air, car and hotel reservations

Contents

Introduction

Gemütlichkeit, a favorite word of the Austrians, conveys the essence of what makes Austria so very special—genuine hospitality combined with old-world charm, cozy ambiance, and country simplicity: all the ingredients that make Austria a treasure just waiting to be discovered. The blend of the Austrians' warmth of welcome and their love of preserving the best of their heritage produces a marvelous travel experience. Best of all, under this happy blanket of gemütlichkeit lies a fascinating country. Many visitors see only Vienna, Salzburg, Innsbruck, and perhaps Kitzbühel, all wonderful towns, but the traveler who returns home without sampling more of this exquisite small country has definitely missed much that Austria has to offer. Read through this guide and see what you might miss. Allocate the time to venture away from the major tourist centers—you will be well rewarded. Live like royalty in a hilltop castle on the Hungarian border; relax in an ancient farmhouse on the shores of the emerald-green Weissensee; pretend you are a child again while riding one of Austria's marvelous little narrow-gauge toy-like trains; slip into the depths of one of Austria's ancient salt mines on a wooden slide worn smooth as silk through years of use; bring your skis and spend your winter holiday in a cozy chalet meeting the challenge of Europe's finest mountain slopes; venture into immense ice caverns where soft lights play magic with frozen fantasies; pack your sturdy shoes and wander over well marked trails into hidden hamlets; climb aboard an old-fashioned ferry and discover quaint villages tucked into tiny coves; relax on a romantic castle terrace overlooking the Danube. The fantasy-land of Austria awaits you.

ABOUT THIS GUIDE

This guide is divided into four sections: practical information useful in planning your trip; five detailed itineraries throughout Austria; a list of a wide selection of hotels with a brief description, an illustration, and pertinent information on each; and maps pinpointing each recommended hotel's location.

We wrote this book with two main objectives: to describe the most charming, small, atmospheric hotels throughout Austria and to tie these hotels together with itineraries that include enough details so that the traveler can plan his own holiday. Any guide that tries to be all things for all people fails. We do not try to give in-depth information on sightseeing—just highlights of some of the most tempting places to see. While traveling you will need to supplement this guide with a detailed reference such as Michelin's *Austria*, an excellent, reliable source for addresses and dates and times museums and other sightseeing venues are open.

We do not try to give a complete listing of hotels in Austria—only the best. We have visited hundreds of hotels and whittled our list down to those we think you will like most. In other words, we have done your homework for you.

Since the hotels included are ones we like, this guide is definitely prejudiced and does not try to appeal to everyone. One of our suggestions might be an elegant castle overlooking the Danube, another a simple, romantic farmhouse nestled by a lake, but there is a common denominator—all the places we recommend have charm. Our theory is that where you stay each night matters and your hotels should add the touch of perfection that makes your holiday very special. The memories you bring home should be more than just of museums, theaters, and tours through palaces. These are important, but this guide takes you through the enchanting back roads of Austria and introduces you to the pleasure of staying in romantic hideaways.

CREDIT CARDS

Many small hotels do not accept credit cards. Those hotels that do accept plastic payment are indicated in the hotel description section using the following abbreviations: AX–American Express, MC–MasterCard, VS–Visa, or simply—all major.

CURRENT

You need a transformer plus an adapter if you plan to take an American-made electrical appliance. The voltage is 220 AC current at 50 cycles/second. Check with the manager of the hotel before plugging anything into an outlet.

DRIVING

BELTS: Seat belts must be worn by everyone in the car. Children under 12 must not sit in the front seat.

DRIVER'S LICENSE: An international driver's license is strongly recommended by the Austrian Tourist Office. This can be purchased for $10 in the USA at your local AAA office. The minimum driving age is 18.

DRUNK DRIVING: It is a very serious offense to drive when you have been drinking. Anyone with an alcohol blood level of 0.8% (less than two beers) is considered under the influence, so do not drink and drive—save your liquid refreshments for evening meals, when your driving is finished for the day.

GASOLINE: Gasoline is very expensive so, if you are driving, budget this as part of your trip's expense. When estimating how much money you will need, figure roughly that gas costs about three times more in Austria than it does in the USA. In addition to the expected combinations of premium and standard gasolines, many stations have another choice where you can create your own mixture to arrive at the perfect octane combination for your car by adjusting the dial on the pump.

PARKING PERMITS: In some cities parking permits are needed for limited-time parking. Cars parked in these special zones need to display in the front window a cardboard clock, available free at gasoline stations, banks, police stations, and tobacco stores. The system is to set the hands of the clock at the time you leave the car so that if a policeman comes by he can check that you have not overstayed your time. Many cities also have paid parking zones. Tickets are available through vending machines in the streets.

ROADS: Most of the major cities are connected by expressways marked by signs showing a double blue line. Traffic moves fast on the expressways where there is a speed limit of 130 kilometers per hour (kph) (one kilometer equals .6 mile.) Highways are also excellent roads, and complete the network. The joy of traveling on these roads is that there is relatively little traffic: of course, the stream of cars increases as you approach major cities, but compared with other European countries the roads are blissfully tranquil. It is rare to be delayed behind a line of cars or a stream of slow-moving trucks. Not to say, though, that you might not have to wait while lines of cows meander across the road on their way home from pasture or slow down for a few kilometers while a farmer drives his tractor back to the farm. The speed limit on highways is 100 kph, in towns 50 kph.

ROAD SIGNS: Before getting on the road, prepare yourself by learning the international driving signs so that you can obey all the rules of the road and avoid the embarrassment and danger of heading the wrong way down a small street or parking in a forbidden area. There are three basic sign shapes: triangular signs warn that there is danger ahead; circular signs indicate compulsory rules and information; square signs give information concerning telephones, parking, camping, etc.

FOOD

Food in Austria is NOT a problem unless you are watching your waistline. You can eat any time, anywhere: it is amazing. Small cafés are found along seemingly deserted mountain paths and warming huts serving an assortment of hot mulled wine, cider, crepes, sausages, soups, and sandwiches are strategically positioned to tempt skiers in from their mountain descent. Even the smallest town is liberally sprinkled with restaurants. In summer, sidewalk terraces magically blossom with tables set with jaunty umbrellas. When you visit Austria be prepared to eat, and eat well.

Breakfast usually consists of a buffet of cheeses, cold meats, cereal, breads, butter, homemade jams, juice and paté, along with a choice of coffee, tea, or hot chocolate. Mid-morning it is tempting to stop for coffee and one of Austria's delectable pastries. Only a few hours after lunch, the cafés are busy again, serving tea and strudel. It is stylish to linger in a coffee house to watch the people and have an ice cream.

Generally the food is excellent. Most countryside inns cultivate small gardens that provide delicious salads and vegetables. Jams are often homemade, breads usually fresh from the oven. Hotel owners are frequently the chefs or, if not, closely supervise the preparation of food. Forget your diet—*mit schlag* (with cream) is the byword in Austria and far too good to pass up. The Austrians use cream on everything—even meat. All your walking will easily compensate for a little indulgence.

A unique Austrian institution is the coffee house. It seems that when the Turks were finally ousted from Austria, in their haste to flee, they left many supplies, including bags of the precious coffee bean. Quick to capitalize on a free gift, a Viennese entrepreneur learned how to prepare his bounty and opened the first Viennese coffee house. Soon the rage spread and coffee houses sprouted up all over the city. The coffee, although superb and served in an astonishingly creative number of ways, is really only incidental: the coffee house serves as a club where friends meet, play chess, read the paper, or just sit and think. Newspapers and magazines are stretched on wooden hangers to be perused leisurely, and games stacked on shelves are for borrowing. The coffee is expensive, but not when you realize what an assortment of pleasures are purchased with one small cup.

Austria is surrounded by seven countries—Germany, Switzerland, Liechtenstein, Italy, Slovenia, Hungary, and the Czech Republic—so it is not surprising that there is such a wonderful selection of cuisine. Austria has absorbed some of the best from each of her neighbors and, with tricks from the kitchen, given them a uniquely Austrian touch. The following list includes some of Austria's most popular foods:

BACKHENDL: Young chickens, breaded and fried to a golden brown.

BREADS: There are too many varieties of delicious breads to list them. Most hotels and restaurants take pride in serving wonderful home-baked breads.

BREGENZERWALD CHEESES: If you follow the *Marvelous Mountains of Tyrol & Vorarlberg* itinerary in this guide, you will travel through the little villages of the Bregenzerwald which produce delicious cheeses.

FRANKFURTER: Contrary to what one would expect, these delicious little sausages originated in Vienna, not in Germany.

GAME: All kinds of game are served and understandably are the specialty of hotels that were once hunting lodges.

GULYA: Goulash served both as a stew and also frequently as a soup—a hearty combination of onions and meat, heavily flavored with paprika.

KARFIOLSUPPE: A thick cauliflower soup.

KNÖDEL: A flour dumpling, flavored with spices and served instead of potatoes with meats, blended with paté and dropped into soups, stuffed with jam and fried, or filled with a sweet fruit and served for dessert.

KRAPFEN: A delicious pastry filled with a sweet fruit filling and then deep-fried.

LEBERKNÖDELSUPPE: A tasty broth with a large paté-flavored dumpling floating in the middle.

PALATSCHINKEN: Thin pancakes sometimes rolled around, or stacked, with a filling such as hazelnuts and topped with whipped cream.

SALAT: Salad is usually a combination of sliced vegetables and greens. However, if you prefer, you can ask for *grüner salat*—green salad.

SALZBURGER NOCKERL: A soufflé made from stiffly beaten eggs and a little flour, served piping hot from the oven and dusted with sugar.

SCHWAMMERLN GEBACKEN: Mushrooms dipped in batter and deep-fried, served with a mayonnaise dill sauce.

STRUDEL: Pie-like pastries with a layered crust. There are many variations of this pastry, the most popular being apple strudel.

TAFELSPITZ: A large piece of beef simmered with herbs and wine until very tender, then sliced and served.

TIROLER GROSTL: Similar to American hash. Cooked beef is cut into small pieces then fried with onions, potatoes, and caraway seed.

TORTE: A layered cake with a wide choice of fillings. The most famous is the Sacher torte, a chocolate cake filled with apricot jam and iced with chocolate.

WIENER SCHNITZEL: Thin fillets of veal, dipped in egg and breadcrumbs then fried to a golden brown.

ZWIEBELROSTBRATEN: Beef steaks which have been hammered thin and then quickly fried on both sides and served with sautéed onion.

Introduction

HISTORY

Read some Austrian history before your holiday—it will make your sightseeing tingle with reality. The rows of portraits in museums will come to life with stories more romantic, more scandalous, more heartwarming than any modern soap opera. There are true stories to appeal to everyone.

What, for example, could touch the heart of every modern woman more than the tale of Maria Theresa, whose portraits and magnificent palaces you will encounter throughout your journey. In 1740, at the age of 23, Maria Theresa assumed the throne of Austria when her father, Charles VI, died unexpectedly. She had absolutely no training for the job and was considered easy prey by the eager politicians just waiting to gain control from this slip of a girl. But she fooled them—and the world. Taking orders from no one, she revitalized the army, built a school system, established Vienna as the center of medicine, reformed the tax laws, created sound economic policies, and negotiated political agreements with neighboring countries—all achieved through a genius for negotiating, reckless courage, and tremendous charm. During her reign, ruling with integrity and compassion, Maria Theresa laid the foundation upon which Austria continued to remain a dominant European power until the first part of the 20th century. She also raised 12 children for whom she arranged royal marriages throughout Europe in hopes of bonding political alliances. The most famous of these arranged marriages was that of her beautiful youngest daughter, Maria Antonia (later called Marie Antoinette), who married the son of Louis XV of France—a marriage whose disastrous results is another chapter in history.

Maria Theresa's story is just one of many equally enticing tales—read, enjoy, and be fortified with information which will add sparkle to your sightseeing.

Introduction

HOTEL DESCRIPTIONS

The third section of this guide lists our recommendations for outstanding places to stay in Austria. We have tried to indicate what each hotel has to offer and to describe the setting, so that you can make the choice to suit your own preferences and vacation. For some of you, cost will not be a factor if the hotel is outstanding; for others, budget will guide your choices; the appeal of a simple little inn with rustic wooden furniture will beckon some, while the glamour of ornate ballrooms dressed with crystal chandeliers and gilt mirrors will appeal to others. We feel that if you know what to expect, you will not be disappointed, so we have tried to be candid and honest in our written appraisals.

All of the hotels featured in this book have been visited and selected solely on their merits. No hotel ever pays to be included. Our judgments are made on charm, setting, cleanliness, and, above all, the warmth of welcome. However, sometimes hotels change. If you find a hotel that is not as we have indicated, please write to us. Also, please let us know if you especially love a hotel we have recommended or have your own discovery to share. Your feedback helps us tremendously in maintaining the quality of our guide.

Austria has a wonderful palette of hotels—delightful lakeside manors, fabulous ski resorts, luxury city hotels, simple farmhouses, fascinating castles—a variety to satisfy the whim and pocketbook of every traveler. Salzburg and Vienna are expensive, though certainly no more so than popular metropolitan areas anywhere in the world. In the countryside the choices are superb and the prices incredibly reasonable, especially in the small country inn or gasthaus. Even though the tab is low, you will frequently find beautiful decor in the dining rooms and linen tablecloths, fresh flowers, and candles on the tables. Normally though, do not expect too much in the bedrooms—usually the antique ambiance is concentrated in the dining rooms, though there are some outstanding exceptions that are noted under the various hotel descriptions. On the following page are descriptions of a sampling of the type of accommodations and hotels you will find in Austria.

CASTLES: Whereas every little village seems to have an inn, every hilltop seems to have a castle. Happily, many of these have been converted into hotels providing some of the best travel buys in Europe. The majority of castle hotels have a faded elegance—those less polite might say a bit shabby. But who could care that the guestrooms are not decorator-perfect when the antique four-poster bed is fit for a king? What does it matter if the Oriental carpet is frayed when the room comes alive with stories of another era

when the countess as a child danced around the Christmas tree? Who can complain if the garden is no longer a spectacle of manicured perfection when photos create visions of a past when beautiful ladies dressed in satin sipped tea on the terrace? There are some castles whose decor is impeccable and whose bathrooms sparkle with all the latest modern fixtures. Castles still owned by the original titled families are often the most interesting. Prices are often amazingly low and with your room comes a slice of romance and history.

FARMHOUSES: Many farmhouses have been turned into inns. These are usually in the country near small towns. Frequently the dining rooms exude a rustic charm with splendid paneling and sturdy little chairs whose backs are carved with hearts. Bedrooms are clean and simple with puffy down comforters on the beds.

HUNTING LODGES: Hunting was the sport for the landed gentry and it seems, in addition to his palace and castle, every nobleman had his own hunting lodge tucked away in the woods. Many of these are now wonderful hotels whose walls are adorned with trophies and a patchwork of photographs hinting at a way of life long gone. Hunting lodges are usually not deluxe. Most of them are quite like they used to be—rustic, simple rooms, lounges where men could sit and discuss the day's hunt, pleasant dining rooms serving an abundance of food (often featuring game, always featuring fresh fruits and vegetables from the garden), guestrooms clean and comfortable but not fancy.

PALACES: Most palaces are located in or near cities and were previously private estates of the nobility. Some are only reflections of the grandeur of the past and could do with a bit of sprucing up, but the price is usually very low, especially considering the romantic atmosphere. Other palaces are superbly maintained, fit for a king, and very expensive.

HOTEL RATES

Each recommended hotel's description includes rates in Austrian shillings (AS). The rates shown are those quoted to us by the hotel for the year 1997 for two persons sharing a room and include breakfast, taxes, and service. These rates are not guaranteed, but rather given as a guideline: it is impossible to cover completely every price possibility because most hotels have an intricate tariff system. **Be sure** to ask at the time of booking the exact price for the room, and what it includes (such as breakfast, tax, etc.).

HOTEL RESERVATIONS

People often ask, "Do I need a hotel reservation?" The answer really depends on how flexible you want to be, how tight your schedule is, which season you are traveling, and how disappointed you would be if your first choice is unavailable.

It is not unusual for the major tourist cities to be completely sold out during the peak season of June through September. Hotel space in the cities is especially crowded, particularly during certain events such as the Music Festival in Salzburg each summer. So unless you don't mind taking your chances on a last-minute cancellation or staying on the outskirts of a town, make a reservation. Space in the countryside is a little easier. However, if you have your heart set on some special little inn, you certainly should reserve as soon as your travel dates are firm.

Reservations are confining. Most hotels will want a deposit to hold your room and frequently refunds are difficult to obtain should you change your plans, especially at the last minute. So it is a double bind: making reservations locks you into a solid framework, but without reservations you might be stuck with accommodations you do not like.

For those who like the security blanket of each night preplanned so that once you leave home you do not have to worry about where to rest your head each night, there are several options for making reservations which we have listed below.

FAX: If you have access to a fax, this is an efficient way to contact a hotel. Many hotels have fax machines, and if so, we give the fax number in the description. The method of faxing is the same as telephoning—dial the international access code (011), followed by the country code for Austria (43), then the city code, followed by the local telephone number. When faxing from anywhere outside of Austria, drop the zero from in front of the city code. (See *Letter* below for suggestions on what to cover in your fax.) Don't forget to include your fax number for their response. At the end of this chapter, on page 27, there is a reservation request letter written in German with an English translation. You can photocopy this to use for either your faxes or letters to Austria. When corresponding with Austria be sure to spell out the month: do not use numbers since in Europe they reverse our system—e.g. 6/9 means September 6 to a European, not June 9.

LETTER: If you start early, you can write to the hotels directly for your reservations. There are certainly many benefits to this in that you can be specific as to your exact preferences. The important point is to be brief in your request. Clearly state the following: number of people in your party; how many rooms you desire; whether you want a private bathroom; date of arrival and date of departure; ask the rate per night and the deposit needed. When you receive a reply, send the deposit and ask for a receipt.

Mail to Europe is sometimes slow so allow about a month for a reply. Although most hotels can understand a letter written in English, at the end of this chapter, on page 27, there is a reservation request letter written in German with an English translation. (See comment above about date.)

TELEPHONE: One of the most satisfactory ways to make a reservation is to call. The cost is minimal if you dial direct and you can have your answer immediately. If space is not available, you can then decide on alternative accommodation. Ask your local operator about the best time to call for the lowest rates. Consider the time change and what time it is in Austria so that you can then call during their business day. Basically, the system is to dial 011, the international code, then 43, Austria's code, followed by the city code and the hotel telephone number which appear under the hotel listings. If you are dialing from outside Austria, omit the initial zero from the city code.

TRAVEL CONSULTANT: A travel consultant can be of great assistance in giving you professional advice and handling all of the details of your holiday. Your travel agent can tie all your arrangements into a neat package, including hotel reservations, airline tickets, boat tickets, train reservations, and sightseeing tours. For your airline tickets there is usually no service fee (unless you are using mileage coupons or some kind of special promotional fare) but most travel agencies do charge for their other services. The best advice is to talk with your local consultant. Be frank about how much you want to spend and ask exactly what he or she can do for you and what the charges will be. If your travel consultant is not familiar with the places in this guide (some are so tiny that they appear in no other major reference source), lend him or her your book—it is written as a guide for travel agents as well as for individual travelers.

USA REPRESENTATIVE: Some hotels in Austria have a United States representative through whom reservations can be made. Many of these representatives have a toll-free telephone number for your convenience. This is an extremely efficient way to secure a reservation. However, if you are on a strict budget, you might find it less expensive to make the reservation yourself since sometimes a representative makes a charge for his service, reserves only the more expensive rooms, or quotes a higher price to protect himself against currency fluctuations and administrative costs. Furthermore, often only the larger or more expensive hotels can afford the luxury of a representative in the United States—so many of the smaller inns must be contacted directly. Nevertheless, this is an excellent way to make a reservation, and United States representatives and their telephone numbers are included in our hotel descriptions. If you plan carefully, you can choose hotels that have the same local representative and one telephone call can complete a bulk of your trip.

We are in no way affiliated with any of the hotels or hotel representatives mentioned in this book, and cannot be responsible for any reservations made nor money sent as deposits or prepayments.

INFORMATION SOURCES

If you have questions not answered in this guide or need special guidance for a particular destination, the Austrian National Tourist Offices can assist you.

Australia: Austrian National Tourist Office, 1st Floor, 36 Carrington St., Sydney NSW 2000, Australia, tel: (2) 299-3621, fax: (2) 299-3808

Canada: Austrian National Tourist Office, 2 Bloor St. E., Suite 3330, Toronto, Ontario M4W 1A8, Canada, tel: (416) 967-3381, fax: (416) 967-4101

England: Austrian National Tourist Office, 30 Saint George St., London W1R 0AL, London, England, tel: (0171) 629-0461, fax: (0171) 499-6038

USA: Austrian National Tourist Office, P.O. Box 1142, New York, NY 10108, USA, tel: (212) 944-6880, fax: (212) 730-4568

Almost all towns throughout Austria have a local tourist office, identified with an "I." We strongly recommend that, during your travels, you make a bee-line to the closest tourist office to check out local events and pick up literature on the area.

ITINERARIES

The second section of this guide outlines itineraries throughout Austria. You should be able to find an itinerary or section of an itinerary to fit your exact time frame and suit your own particular interests. You can custom-tailor your own itinerary by combining segments of itineraries or using two back to back. The itineraries do not indicate a specific number of nights at each destination, since to do so seemed much too confining. Again, personality dictates what is best for a particular situation: some travelers like to see as much as possible in a short period of time and do not mind rising with the birds each morning to begin a new adventure, while for others, just the thought of packing and unpacking each night makes them shudder in horror and they would never stop for less than three or four nights at any one destination. A third type of tourist does not like to travel at all—the destination is the focus and he will use this guide to find the perfect spot from which he will never wander except for daytime excursions.

Use this guide as a reference from which to plan your very own personalized trip. We cannot, however, help adding our recommendation: do not rush. Learn to travel as the Europeans do and don't try to do too much. Pick out a place to stay that especially appeals to you and just relax, using your hotel as a hub for exploring the surrounding countryside. Allow sufficient time to enjoy and absorb the special ambiance each hotel has to offer. One proprietor commented that Americans travel so fast they do not always remember where they are, and told the story of stopping to see if she could assist an American woman studying her map in great frustration on a street corner in Vienna. She asked if she could help, only to find the poor lady was looking for St. Mark's Square in Venice!

MAPS

MAPS–ITINERARY: With each itinerary there is a map showing the routing and suggesting places of interest along the way. These are an artist's renderings and are not intended to replace a good commercial map. To supplement our routings you will need a set of detailed maps which will indicate all of the highway numbers, expressways, alternative little roads, expressway access points, exact distances, etc. Our suggestion is to purchase a comprehensive selection of both city maps and regional maps before your departure, and with a highlight pen mark your own personalized itinerary and pinpoint your city hotels. (Note: Frequently in Austria the hotels do not have a street address—especially in small towns, the town itself is the only address. However, in most cases the tourist bureau does an excellent job of placing signs strategically to guide the tourist to each of the hotels once you are close.) Be sure to get a map that has an index with it. Our preference for maps are those by Freytag & Berndt who make a series of five maps that are very detailed, have an index, and cover all of Austria. Map 1 covers Vienna, Upper Austria, and Lower Austria; Map 2 covers Styria and Carinthia; Map 3 covers Tyrol and Vorarlberg; Map 4 covers Salzburg and Salzkammergut; Map 5 covers Lower Austria, Vienna, and part of Burgenland. Bookstores can usually order maps for you if they do not have them in stock.

MAPS–HOTEL LOCATIONS: In the *Maps* section (the last section of this book) there is a key map of the whole of Austria plus seven regional maps showing each recommended hotel's position. In order to find which of our regional maps highlights the town where your hotel is located, the pertinent map number is shown on the *top line* of each hotel's description. To further ease the task of spotting the town, we divided the hotel location maps into a grid of four parts. The upper left segment is designated "a," the upper right segment "b," the lower left segment "c," and the lower right segment "d."

MAPS–PROVINCES:

Austria is divided into nine regions, or provinces, one of which is a very small area that encircles the city of Vienna and another small area, defined as East Tyrol, is actually part of the larger province, Tyrol. Some of the provinces have two completely different spellings—one in English, the other in German, and you will see both referenced. In German, the provinces are referred to as Länder and the translation for the regions is as follows: Burgenland is Burgenland, Carinthia is Kärnten, Lower Austria is Niederösterreich, Upper Austria is Oberösterreich, Salzburg is Salzburgerland, Styria is Steiermark, Tyrol is Tirol, (East-Tyrol, a district of Tyrol, is Öst Tirol), Vienna is Wien, and Vorarlberg is Vorarlberg.

Provinces of Austria

MUSIC

Many of the world's greatest musical geniuses were born within a few miles of Vienna. Incredibly, they were all born within a relatively short span of history and their lives and music were interrelated. Haydn, Mozart, Liszt, Strauss, Schubert, and Bruckner are just a few of the men whose musical compositions have added so much joy to the world. No one knows for sure what caused this sublime surge of talent. Many experts think it was probably due to the Austrians' innate love of music and to the fact that it was the style

for the wealthy nobility to sponsor musical genius—in much the same way that the Italian aristocracy sponsored artists. Whatever the reason, the world is much richer thanks to these sons of Austria. Reading their biographies and listening to their music will greatly add to the enjoyment of your holiday.

SHOPPING

Most shops are open from 9 am to 6 pm, and closed for an hour or two in the middle of the day when the shopkeeper goes home for lunch. In resort areas, some of the shops are open seven days a week, but in most towns the stores are closed Saturday afternoons and

Sundays. The shops are filled with many tantalizing items attractively and artfully displayed.

Described below and on the following pages are some of the favorite items to take home.

CERAMICS: Ceramics are made in Gmunden, which is in the lake district near Salzburg. You can buy anything from an entire dinner set to a beer mug. If your itinerary does not take you to Gmunden, take heart: the ceramics are also available in shops in Salzburg, Vienna, and Innsbruck.

DIRNDLS: Dirndls are charming pinafores usually of provincial-print material worn with a white blouse and apron. All sizes are available from adorable tiny dresses for little girls to matching costumes for mom and grandmother. In addition to all sizes, the dresses come in all fabrics and designs from gay daytime cotton models to fabulous pure silk high-fashion designer creations.

GLASSWARE: In the medieval town of Rattenburg, along the Inn river near Innsbruck, you can buy from a wonderful selection of glasses of all kinds. These are made by local craftsmen who came from Czechoslovakia as refugees and brought their craft with them. You can have your glassware engraved while you wait or have it mailed home.

LEATHER GOODS: The leather in Austria is especially beautiful: not only is it soft and lovely, but also skillfully styled. The skirts and jackets are expensive, but absolutely gorgeous.

LEDERHOSEN: A trip to Austria would not be complete without bringing home a pair of wonderful leather shorts for all the men and little boys in the family. They are not expensive and just do not wear out.

PETITPOINT: Vienna is famous for its beautiful petitpoint needlework which is available in handbags, eyeglass cases, belts, etc. There are many cheap imitations in the souvenir shops, but the real thing is very expensive and very exquisite.

SKI EQUIPMENT: The ski equipment in Austria does not seem any great buy; however, it is fun to bring home a pair of skis or boots, if for no other reason than the memory, especially if you were on a ski holiday.

SWEATERS: There are many beautiful woolen sweaters for men, women, and children. Especially comfortable, and typically Austrian, are the sweaters which look like jackets.

TEXTILES: Austria has lovely materials. The country motif designs are popular and make beautiful curtains, tablecloths, napkins, etc.

TYROLEAN HATS: It is fun to bring home a jaunty Austrian felt hat.

WOODEN BOXES: Wooden boxes of all sizes and styles, painted with gay Tyrolean designs of flowers and hearts, are available.

If you are going to do much shopping, be aware that there are substantial savings available on a tax credit plan. If you buy over 1,000 shillings'-worth of goods at the same store, you can get a 13% tax refund. Not all stores participate in the program, so when shopping, ask if the store does. If it does, ask for a tax refund form which the store will fill out. As you leave the European Union you *must* have this form stamped by the tax inspector at the airport or border crossing. If you are leaving by train, you must get off the train at the border and have the inspector at the customs office stamp the form and the receipts. Keep your purchases together because the customs agent will probably want to see what you have bought. If leaving from the airport go to the airport customs office. You can receive an immediately refund in cash from the tax-free refund counter. There are also tax-free refund facilities available at some road border crossings. You can also mail your tax-free cheque back to Austria in pre-addressed envelopes not later than 60 days from the date of purchase. If returning to Austria, you can go back to the store and they will reimburse the tax you paid. Most of the stores give you an information sheet that explains all the different places you can receive the refunds.

If you are not a resident of one of the EU countries and the total value of goods purchased in a shop displaying the "tax-free for tourists" sign, ask for a tax-free cheque to be issued, along with the regular receipt for your purchase. Goods must be purchased at an affiliated retail outlet with the "tax-free for tourists" sign.

TRANSPORTATION

BOATS: Most lakes have ferryboats which operate from spring to fall, and there is no lovelier way to explore Austria's lakes than from the deck of a boat. No reservations are needed and the schedule is always posted at the pier. Be sure to be on time because the boats glide in and out of the docks like clockwork and passengers who are late are left behind.

A popular boat excursion is the ferryboat which plies the Danube between Passau and Vienna. If you wish to take just a segment between these two towns, you need no reservation: simply buy your ticket and climb aboard. However, if you are taking the entire trip and desire a cabin, then reservations are needed in advance. These ferries are not deluxe, but lots of fun and a marvelous way to see the countryside.

Another option is to take the hydrofoil which links Vienna with Budapest. The trip to Budapest takes four-and-a-half hours, the return trip takes five-and-a-half. Reservations should be made in advance.

TRAINS: Austria has excellent trains and a spiderweb of routes which link most of the cities and small towns. For train buffs there is another wonderful option—nostalgic narrow-gauge trains (some still with steam engines) that take passengers into some of the most beautiful and remote areas of Austria. Originally these were built by the emperor so that he could keep in contact with people living in isolated mountain regions. Later, after roads were built, many of the trains remained—a reminder of a romantic past. These trains look too cute to be real. As you are driving along, you will hear a "toot toot" and winding through the valley will be a gay little engine pulling a stream of brightly painted cars loaded with passengers.

On some of these trains you can even be the conductor and command the train from a perch in the engine, although your conductor's status must usually be reserved in advance. For further information concerning when and where these "toy" trains operate, contact the Austrian National Tourist Office, P.O. Box 1142, New York, NY 10108, tel: (212) 944-6880, or fax: (212) 730-4568.

Most train stations have a desk where someone speaks English to assist you with schedules. If you are traveling extensively on trains, you might consider buying a comprehensive publication, *Fahrplane*, available at any train station. This publication has a map and all the schedules for trains, boats, and buses.

On international trains that whip between European countries you frequently need to reserve a seat in advance, and you need to pay a supplement on some express trains. However, for local trains you pay no supplement and rarely need a seat reservation—if you have a ticket, just hop aboard and find a seat. The cars are marked on the outside first or second class and within both categories there are designated smoking and non-smoking seating areas. Some of the trains have dining cars, some have a person who walks through selling snacks, and some have no food service.

For trains within Austria you can either purchase individual, point-to-point tickets or use a pass. Eurailpasses are valid in Austria (one of the 17 European countries on the Eurailpass system) or, once you arrive in Austria, you might want to buy a *bundes-netzkarte*, a one-month rail pass that can be purchased only within the country. The *bundes-netzkarte* costs AS 5,400 (approximately $570) for first class and AS 3,600 (approximately $380) for second class. There is also the *kilometerbank* card which also can be purchased only within Austria. This is a card printed with 2,000, 3,000, or 5,000 kilometers and can be used by up to six friends or family traveling together. The conductor deducts the appropriate distance used depending upon the length of the trip. The 2,000-kilometer card costs AS 2,300 (approximately $242), the 3,000-kilometer card costs AS 3,450 (approximately $363), and the 5,000-kilometer card costs AS 5,750 (approximately $605).

To make your journey more carefree, there are several terms you should be able to recognize when you are in the train stations. With these few terms you should be in business.

BAHNHOF: Train station

SCHIFFAHRT: Boat dock

STANDSEILBAHN: Cable car

KABINENSEILBAHN: Gondola

ABFAHRT: Time of departure

NACH: Traveling to

BAHNSTEIG: Platform number at the train station

GLEIS: Track number.

WEATHER

Austria's weather is fickle. There is rain. Lots of rain. It can be pouring in the morning, and be a beautiful sunny day by noon. Do not count on warm days: consider yourself lucky if it is balmy and be prepared for chilly weather with sweaters that can be pulled off as the day warms. You may be lucky and have your entire holiday a collection of perfect days, but as you admire the incredibly green fields and splendid array of flowers, your common sense will tell you that this lush splendor is not the result of a man-made irrigation system. Be prepared with the proper clothing and enjoy Austria rain or shine, snow or sun, cold or warm.

WHAT TO WEAR

For winter bring warm coats, sweaters, gloves, snug hats, and boots. The rest of the year a layered effect will equip you for any kind of weather: skirts or trousers combined with blouses or shirts that can then be built upon with layers of sweaters depending upon the chill of the day. A raincoat is a must, along with a folding umbrella. Sturdy, comfortable walking shoes are recommended not only for roaming the many beckoning mountain trails, but also for negotiating cobbled streets. Daytime dress is casual, but in the evening it is appropriate to dress for dinner. Nothing elaborate is necessary, just a sport coat and tie for men and a dress or sweater and skirt for women. It is a courtesy to the hotels to change into more formal attire in the evenings when dining in their restaurants.

WINES

Although not as well-known as those of France, Germany, and Italy, Austrian wines are delicious and plentiful. The majority of grapes are grown in Lower Austria, but vineyards are also found in the provinces of Burgenland, Vienna, and Styria. Wine labels usually indicate the region of their origin and the grape variety. There is no single "wine road" in Austria as there is in Germany, but a series of short excursions in various areas will be rewarding for the wine enthusiast. In Lower Austria the Wachau provides a delightful 48-kilometer stretch of terraced vineyards which line the steep banks of the Danube as it winds its way between Melk and Krems.

Another lovely route is found near the Hungarian border, where fabulous wines are grown around the charming old town of Rust. Another popular wine area is in the rolling hills around Vienna. *Heurigen* are simple homes or little shops whose proprietors offer for sale the wines from the previous year's harvest. A branch of greenery is hung over the door to announce to all that wine sampling is available inside. Often tables are set

outside on a vine-covered terrace where light snacks are also served. To complete the enjoyment, there is often music and singing. There are many popular heurigen near Vienna, but many of these have become a bit trite with the arrival of busloads of tourists. Most fun are the "real" heurigen in the countryside—frequently in the home of a vintner who opens his doors to the public and serves his latest wines accompanied by simple food. Heurigen date back to the 18th century when Joseph II ruled that individual vintners could sell their own wines privately.

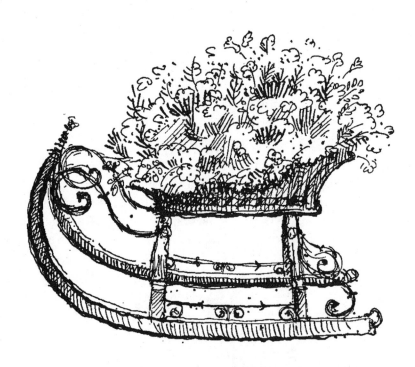

RESERVATION REQUEST LETTER

HOTEL NAME & ADDRESS

Ich möchte anfragen:　　　　　I would like to request:

Number of double rooms with private bath/shower
____ (No. of double rooms)*Doppelzimmer mit Bad/Dusche*

Number of single rooms with private bath/shower
____ (No. of single rooms)*Einzelzimmer mit Bad/Dusche*

Number of persons in our party
Wir sind ____ (No. of persons) *Personen*

Arrival date
Wir kommen am _____ *an* (Day/Month/Year, spell out month)

Departure date
Wir reisen am _____ *an* (Day/Month/Year, spell out month)

Please let me know as soon as possible the following:
Bitte lassen Sie mich so bald wie möglich wissen:

Can you reserve the space requested?　　　Yes　　　　　No
Ob Sie die angefragten Zimmer haben?　　*Ja* ____　　____ *Nein*

Rate per room per night?
Der Preis pro Zimmer / Nacht?

Are meals included in your rate?　　　　Yes　　　　　No
Sind Mahlzeiten in diesem Preis enthalten?　*Ja* ____　　____ *Nein*

Do you need a deposit?　　　　　　　Yes　　　　　No
Benötigen Sie eine Anzahlung?　　　*Ja* ____　　____ *Nein*

How much deposit do you need?
Wenn ja, wie hoch ist die Anzahlung?

Thank you, and Best Regards,

Vielen Dank im voraus. Mit freundlichen Grüssen, YOUR NAME & ADDRESS

Salzburg

Highlights of Austria by Train and Boat–or Car

CZECH REPUBLIC

SLOVAKIA

GERMANY

Dürnstein
LINZ   Weissenkirchen   Krems
Steyr   Danube   VIENNA
Amstetten   Melk

SALZBURG
Hof

Hungerburg
Brixlegg
Berwang   Goldegg am See
KITZBÜHEL   Schwarzach/ St.Veit
Feldkirch   Zell am See
Lech   Imst   INNSBRUCK
Oetz   Lans   Badgastein
Patsch

Bruck

GRAZ

Millstätter See
Mallnitz   St Veit
Weissensee   Pörtschach   Burg Hochosterwitz
am Wörther See
KLAGENFURT   HUNGARY

SWITZERLAND   ITALY
Villach
Velden   Maria Wörth

SLOVENIA

◉ Suggested Overnight Stops
∗ Alternate Hotel Choices
○ Orientation/Sightseeing
— By Train
= By Boat
▰ Borders
--- Tunnel

29

Highlights of Austria by Train & Boat–or Car

Many travelers long for the freedom to travel at their own pace, to choose their own hotels, and to avoid the confinement of a packaged tour, but their sense of adventure does not quite extend to driving in a foreign country. If this dilemma applies to you, do not despair: Austria's public transportation is convenient, well organized, moderate in price, and, best of all—fun. Such fun in fact that many of you who usually rent a car might want to consider making this vacation a complete holiday for all, including the driver, and choose to see Austria by train and boat. To climb aboard a train or boat immediately evokes a mood of romance, a twinge of nostalgia. As you whiz through meadows of wildflowers, chug over mountain passes, zip through tunnels, trace narrow gorges, or float lazily down the Danube, the world is yours. Transportation of this kind is not a means to an end: it is a sightseeing adventure. This itinerary covers some of Austria's highlights—an excellent choice for seeing Austria for the first time whether you follow the itinerary by train and boat—or car.

Dürnstein

This itinerary can easily be duplicated by car, in which case you do not need to be overly concerned with luggage. However, should you choose to travel by train and boat, you really must travel lightly. To lug a heavy suitcase from train to taxi to hotel soon dims your joy, and the journey becomes drudgery. But if each person has just one small suitcase (preferably on wheels), freedom and adventure are yours.

IMPORTANT NOTE: Times are given as a reference so that you can see how the pieces of the itinerary fit together and gauge the approximate time to allow between destinations. Since schedules constantly change, especially between seasons, please verify each of the times. At train stations you can pick up handy, free, easy-to-read, small pocket-sized schedules for specific train routes. These pamphlets also list connecting trains to other major cities. Also every station has an information desk with an English-speaking agent who can assist you with train schedules.

ORIGINATING CITY   SALZBURG

Salzburg is a medieval town that snuggles in a small pocket of land, traced on one side by the Salzach river and hemmed in on the other by the Mönchberg, a small mountain that rises steeply from the city. Salzburg has a story-book quality with narrow streets, colorful old houses, charming little squares, arcaded courtyards, and enticing shops. Always a special favorite of tourists is the **Getreidegasse**, a picturesque street lined by buildings that are accented by whimsical wrought-iron signs. Salzburg is so charming you can spend hours just meandering through the maze of streets which frequently converge like spokes into small squares. It is easy to get lost, but the town is so small that you can quickly find a familiar landmark and be on your way again.

When you settle down to sightseeing, you will be pleased to discover that most places of interest are within easy walking distance. Be sure not to miss any of the following: the intriguing fortress, **Hohensalzburg**, which looms above the city and is reached by funicular from the edge of town; **Saint Peter's Abbey**, a Benedictine abbey which (until

Getreidegasse, Salzburg

1110) was the archbishops' residence; the 17th-century **Salzburg Cathedral**, modeled after Saint Peters in Rome, which has over four thousand pipes in its organ and three massive bronze doors representing "Faith," "Love," and "Hope"; the **Glockenspiel** whose 36 bells play Mozart tunes at 7 am, 11 am, and 6 pm; the **Residenze**, an opulent palace, once home to the wealthy prince bishops, whose lavish apartments and art gallery (with a wealth of 16- to 19th-century paintings) are open to the public; and **Mozart's birthplace**, now a museum filled with portraits, musical scores, keyboard instruments, and violins. Just across the river from the heart of Old Salzburg—an easy walk over the pedestrian bridge—are the **Mirabell Gardens** which you must not miss. The Schloss Mirabell and the Mirabell gardens were built in 1606 by Archbishop Wolf Dietrich for his mistress, Salome Alt. As you walk through enchanting terraced lawns you can imagine the Archbishop strolling with his "favorite" while their children romped nearby.

Before arriving in Salzburg check with the Austrian National Tourist Office to see what special events are happening during your visit. A popular event in late summer (last week in July through August) is the **Salzburg Music Festival**, featuring opera, chamber music, concerts, and many world-renowned artists. Should your visit coincide with this event, you will need to plan far in advance—not only for tickets, but also for hotel space. (Note: Unless you are an ardent music lover, avoid Salzburg during the music festival since the city is crowded and hotel prices soar.)

One event you must include is the **Marionette Opera,** with performances taking place from Easter through September in the Marionetten Theater, which is located near the Mirabell Gardens. The marionettes usually perform Mozart operas. The exquisite scenery, splendid marionettes dressed in intricate costumes, and the agility and talent of the skillful fingers manipulating the strings combine to make a magical evening you will long remember. Arrive early so that you can spend time studying the showcases of marionettes from past performances. Their tiny costumes of fine silks, handmade laces, velvets, and feathers are amazing.

There are many excellent day trips available from Salzburg. One of the tours takes in the beautiful lakes and towering Dachstein mountains—this area is called the **Salzkammergut.** Other tours go to the salt mines—the name of Salzburg evolves from *salz* (salt) and *burg* (fortress). The mining of salt was responsible for Salzburg's wealth and power and the mines can still be visited, making an exciting tour. There are also ice caves near Salzburg—a beautiful outing not only because the caves are fascinating with their fabulous formations of ice, but the scenery is exceptionally lovely too. Another favorite day tour is *The Sound of Music*, a bus tour that visits the landmarks in and around Salzburg where the movie was filmed.

Salzburg has an abundant selection of hotels in all price ranges. Some are in the heart of the city, others in the suburbs within easy driving distance (or in some cases convenient to public transportation). The hotel section describes the various recommendations.

DESTINATION I   DÜRNSTEIN

It is a short cab ride from the center of Old Salzburg to the train station. On rainy days it sometimes takes ten or fifteen minutes just to summon a cab, so allow plenty of time. Your train journey takes you from Salzburg to Melk, a boat station for the Danube ferry. Melk has a marvelous Benedictine abbey which dominates the hill above the town and overlooks the river and those who want to visit the abbey should leave Salzburg on the early-morning train. However, if you prefer to get a more leisurely start, you can forego the abbey and take a later train. Trains leave every hour for Amstetten with a connection to Melk.

8:10 am Leave Salzburg by train
10:16 am Arrive Amstetten

10:45 am Leave Amstetten by train
11:23 am Arrive Melk

After leaving Salzburg station it is only minutes until you are out of the city and surrounded by the beautiful hills and lakes which make the area around Salzburg so famous. The landscape is lovely, with high mountains in the distance and rolling low hills dotted with farms in the foreground. As the train nears Linz, industrial areas begin to appear, but once you are through the city the scenery is again one of pastoral beauty. As you near **Melk** watch closely, for you will have a beautiful view of **Melk Abbey**.

When you arrive in Melk, a five-minute taxi ride takes you to the ferry stop. There are two docks, one for the large ferry which goes between Passau and Vienna and another for the local ferry. If the taxi driver does not speak English (and you are not fluent in

German), jot down on a slip of paper "Schiffahrt—Wien." This will tell him that you want the boat dock for the ferry going to Vienna.

At the boat dock purchase a ticket to Vienna, which allows you a free stopover at tonight's destination, Dürnstein. Once you have your ticket, check your bags so that you are free to walk around until the boat arrives. There is a baggage room at the ticket office—if it is closed, the person who sells the tickets will open it for you. There is a nice restaurant with a pleasant riverfront terrace just a two-minute walk from the dock. If you are not visiting the abbey, this makes a great spot to relax while waiting for the ferry.

As the time for the ferry's arrival draws near, people suddenly congregate. The recently deserted dock teems with activity: young boys with bicycles, families with picnic baskets, hikers in sturdy shoes with knapsacks on their shoulders, busloads of tourists. Once on board, stake your claim and find a table and some chairs where you can enjoy the journey. The ferry has a dining room and several snack bars.

2:00 pm Leave Melk by Danube ferry
3:25 pm Arrive Dürnstein

The section of the Danube between Melk and Dürnstein is very famous and very beautiful. During these few kilometers, the river lazily loops and turns as it cuts its way through the hills that sometimes rise so precipitously as to give a fjord-like beauty. This is the famous **Wachau** region of Austria whose grapes produce some of the country's finest wines. Along the banks of the river, vineyards terrace up the steep hillsides, small wine-producing villages nestle at every hospitable spot on the shore, and romantic ruins of castles pierce the skyline. En route the major points of interest are pointed out in English.

Your destination is the enchanting village of **Dürnstein**. This tiny hamlet, perched on a ledge overlooking the Danube, is fairy-tale-perfect. Still walled, the village boasts colorful houses, a tiny square, a lovely monastery with an especially attractive courtyard, and the ruins of a castle atop the hill. The castle has its own fairy tale: in 1192 Leopold V captured England's King Richard the Lionheart and hid him in **Dürnstein Castle**. No one knew where the king was imprisoned. Blondel, the King's devoted minstrel, devised a plan to find his master and drifted from castle to castle playing King Richard's favorite songs. When Blondel reached Dürnstein, he played and sang beneath the castle walls. Richard recognized the voice of his minstrel and joined in the singing, which led to his rescue. As in all fairy tales, the story had a happy ending!

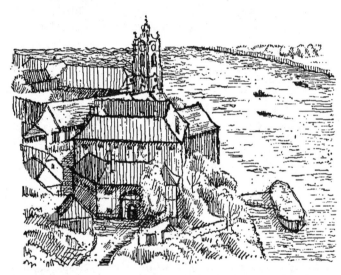

Schloss Dürnstein,
Dürnstein

We recommend two places to stay in Dürnstein (both described in detail in the hotel section). The first, **Schloss Dürnstein**, is one of our favorite hotels in Austria. This beautifully furnished, romantic hotel is built into the old town walls and has a tranquil terrace where you can dine outside while enjoying a stunning view of the river. Our other recommendation, the **Gasthof "Sänger Blondel"** (a less expensive hotel tucked into the center of the village) offers great warmth of welcome and charm. If you advise either of the hotels when you will arrive, they will send a porter to the pier to help you with your luggage and guide you to your hotel.

Dürnstein is so small that it takes only a short walk to explore it from one gate to the other. Nevertheless, Dürnstein is so romantic that it would make a wonderful stopover for a few days. There are many paths to explore, including a walk to Weissenkirchen, another beautiful old wine village located about 4 kilometers away. With careful planning you can hike to Weissenkirchen and return by ferry to Dürnstein.

DESTINATION II   VIENNA

Dürnstein makes a good base for enjoying this beautiful region of Austria. When it is time to leave, a porter will carry your bags to the pier. It is possible to take a train from Krems (about a 7-kilometer taxi ride from Dürnstein) to Vienna, but the ferry is more fun. You can check out of your hotel and leave your luggage at the front desk while you enjoy a last stroll through town and a lingering lunch before leaving.

4:10 pm Leave Dürnstein by ferry
8:15 pm Arrive Vienna

The first town you come to is **Krems**. As you near the town, watch for the magnificent Benedictine monastery, **Gottweig Abbey**, which dominates the top of a hill. Although it is far in the distance on the right bank of the river, it appears quite dramatic and beautiful in the late afternoon sunlight due to its immense size. After Krems, the banks of the river flatten out and become less scenic, but before you have time to become restless, you arrive at an enormous lock which drops the boat from the high level of a dam to the lower flow of the river below. It is fascinating to watch the boat sink about 12 meters and, as the gates slowly swing open, glide out into the river below. Beyond the lock you will see on the right a large nuclear power station which, although finished for several years, has never been put into operation. There is a second lock to navigate before you see the distant skyline of **Vienna**.

Since the ferry does not arrive in Vienna until evening, it is wise to have dinner before the boat docks. The ferry's dining room has large windows, so you do not miss any of the action as you enjoy your meal.

Upon arrival in Vienna, take a cab to your hotel. In the hotel section in the back of the book we recommend a selection of places to stay in every price range, from luxury hotels to simple pensions. Read the descriptions carefully and you should find a hotel that suits you perfectly.

There is so much to see and do in Vienna that it almost demands a book in itself. Although this is a spread-out metropolis, most of the sightseeing attractions are in the heart of the city bound by the Ringstrasse, a loop of roads built where the medieval walls of the city once existed. If you enjoy walking, most of the places of interest are easily accessibly by foot. (Those outside the inner city can be visited by bus tours or on the subway.)

Buy a city map and a sightseeing guide. To get acquainted with the major points of interest, take a city tour and then go back to savor at length your favorite museums, cathedrals, and palaces. There are many tour operators and your hotel will have their brochures. However, if there are several persons in your party, check the price of a private car with English-speaking guide. You can cover so much more of the city and squeeze so much more information into a small amount of time when you do not have to wait for a busload of other passengers and a private car does not cost much more if you have several persons to share the expense. You will certainly want to see all of the following places of interest.

The **Vienna State Opera House** is renowned throughout the world. Opened in May 1869, the beautiful Renaissance-style building faces the Ringstrasse. Although badly damaged during World War II, it was rebuilt to duplicate its original grandeur. In July and August, and even when performances are not being held during the opera season from September through June, the Opera House is open for tours. It is great fun to take the tour and see behind the scenes of this spectacular building.

The **Hofburg Palace** (frequently called just *die Burg*) is much more than a palace. Although it was indeed the home of the Hapsburgs until 1918, it is actually an enormous complex of gardens, museums, and theaters. You could easily spend several days here enjoying the wealth of sightseeing possibilities which include the following places of great interest. The **Spanish Riding School** (*Spanische Hofreitschule*), founded in 1572, is where the gorgeous white **Lippizaner stallions** display their incredible talents, dancing to classical music in an opulent 18th-century ballroom, painted white and hung with crystal chandeliers. Performances take place from March through June and from September to mid-December on Sundays at 10:45 am and Wednesdays at 7 pm. If you cannot see one of the performances, you can watch one of the training sessions. These take place from mid-February to June, from the end of August until mid-October, and again from mid-November to mid-December, Tuesdays through Saturdays at 10 am. (Open year-round is a small museum where you can view samples of the ornate riding costumes and a video showing the history of the riding school.)

Just across the square from the riding school is the **Augustinian Church** (*Augustinerkirche*). This exquisite church dates back to the 14th century and the Sunday morning high mass at 11 am is truly memorable. Many famous events have taken place here including the wedding of Maria Theresa to François of Lorraine and the wedding of her daughter, Marie-Louise, to Louis XVI of France. In the **Imperial Apartments**

(*Kaiserappartements*), once the royal residence, you can imagine the opulent lifestyle of the ruling family. The **Imperial Treasury** (*Schatzkammer*) displays the kingdom's crown jewels. Among the dazzling treasures on display is a magnificent 1,000-year-old crown studded with diamonds, emeralds, sapphires, and rubies. (This crown was stolen by Hitler, but returned to Austria after the war.)

The **New Château** (*Neue Burg*), once the residence of Archduke Franz Ferdinand, now houses several spectacular museums. In one wing you can see one of the world's most extensive collections of weapons and armor, while another wing has a marvelous **Museum of Musical Instruments** (*Musikinstrumentensammlung*) where you can wander through room after room of musical instruments dating from the 16th to 18th centuries. (Be sure to take one of the headphones that play the music of the period as you enjoy the beautiful instruments.) Also in the New Château is the **Ephesos Museum** which displays artifacts from ancient Greece and Turkey and the **Ethnographical Museum** (*Museum für Völkerkunde*) which displays some fabulous pre-Columbian artifacts including an incredible authentic Aztec feather headdress. Another museum in the New Château is the **Austrian National Library** (*Österreichische Nationalbibliothek*), one of the most impressive and beautiful libraries in the world with a collection of rare manuscripts dating back to the 14th century. The New Château also houses the 15th-century **Palace Chapel** (*Burgkapelle*) where the world-famous **Vienna Boys' Choir** performs. Performances are given January through June and mid-September until the end of December at 9:15 am. Reservations must be made far in advance by writing to: Verwaltung der Hofmusikkapelle, Hofburg, 1010, Vienna, Austria.

One of the most elegant shopping streets in Europe is the Kärthner Strasse, a pedestrian-only avenue that runs from the Opern Ring to Stephansplatz where you find one of Vienna's landmarks, **Saint Stephen's Cathedral**, (*Dompfarre St. Stephan*). You must not miss seeing this richly adorned cathedral with its dramatic Gothic tower soaring 137 meters into the sky, one of Vienna's landmarks.

There are two palaces you must visit that are outside the heart of the city, but easily accessible. The first of these is the beautiful **Schönbrunn Palace** with its **Schönbrunn Gardens**. Reached from the center of Vienna by the U4 subway, the Schönbrunn Palace is well worth the journey. This huge palace (1,400 rooms) was the summer home of the Hapsburg family and now 40 of its rooms are open to the public (including the impressive Hall of Mirrors where the six-year-old Mozart played for Maria Theresa). Although the palace is a masterpiece, the spectacular formal gardens that surround it are truly sensational. Also outside the heart of Vienna is the **Belvedere Palace**. Actually two palaces joined by extensive gardens, the Beleve Palace was built in the 18th century as a summer home of Prince Eugene of Savoy.

In addition to the endless variety of castles, museums, palaces, gardens, parks, churches, and entertainment to be savored within Vienna, on the outskirts of the city you can enjoy a trip to the beautiful **Vienna Woods,** or a trip to **Mayerling** where the tragic Prince Rudolph, only son of the Emperor Franz Joseph, committed suicide with his young mistress, Baroness Vetsera, in 1889. Or travel to **Grinzing** to sample the new wines and join in with the music and gaiety. There is so much to see and do in Vienna that you could spend your entire holiday here.

When you begin to plan your holiday, contact the Austrian National Tourist Office (see page 14 for details) to find out what will be highlighted while you are visiting and how to obtain tickets for performances. Tickets for the Opera, the Spanish Riding School, and Vienna Boys' Choir must be purchased far in advance. Note: Some hotels will also make reservations for you for the special events—ask when you book your hotel room.

Highlights of Austria by Train & Boat–or Car   41

After a busy sightseeing schedule, it will be a pleasant contrast to spend a few days in the south beside one of Austria's loveliest lakes, the Wörther See. The train connections are easy and the ride is especially beautiful. You depart from the South Station (*Südbahnhof*), about a five-minute taxi ride from the Palais Schwarzenberg.

10:55 am Leave Vienna South Station by train
3:32 pm Arrive Pörtschach am Wörther See

Leaving Vienna, the land is flat as you pass through small suburbs and commercial areas, but within an hour the panorama from your window becomes enchanting—beautiful wooded hills, lush green meadows, castles dotting mountaintops, rocky cliffs, small villages, and tiny chapels. You will not want to take your eyes from the window for fear of missing a magnificent castle partially hidden behind giant trees or an exquisite onion-domed little chapel on a mountain ledge. In a couple of hours the train will arrive in Bruck an der Mur which is a small industrial town at the junction of the Murz and Mur rivers. The train follows the River Mur west from Bruck. For a short while the scene is industrial but soon the suburbs are behind you and you enter a serene rural area—a wide valley filled with fields of wheat and enclosed by forested hills. Cows graze in square patches of meadow amongst the trees on the rolling hills. About an hour from Bruck the train makes a curve to the south and heads for the large city of **Klagenfurt**. Watch closely because about 15 minutes before the train comes to Klagenfurt, near the town of Saint Veit an der Glan, you will see on the left side of the train **Burg Hochosterwitz**, a fascinating castle dominating the top of a miniature mountain. After leaving Klagenfurt, the train follows the lake and in a few minutes you are in **Pörtschach**.

We recommend two hotels in Pörtschach: the super-deluxe **Schloss Seefels**, sitting directly on the lake just west of town, and the charming **Schloss Leonstein**, located in the center of town. Details on both can be found in the hotel section.

Maria Wörth, Wörther See

The Wörther See is a lovely lake backdropped by majestic mountains. While staying in Pörtschach be sure to take one of the ferries that ply the lake—the complete circle takes several hours. It is fun to get off in one of the villages en route, do a little exploring, then board another ferry to continue your journey. The most attractive of the towns is **Maria Wörth**, on a peninsula that juts into the lake. A beautiful Gothic parish church crowns the crest of the hill in the center of the village and makes a splendid picture as the boat draws near.

In addition to a lake excursion, there are many package bus tours you can take from Pörtschach. One you should not miss is to **Burg Hochosterwitz**, the castle you saw earlier from the train. Be sure to wear sturdy shoes because you have to walk up to the castle, built on what looks like a toy mountain. The path zigzags up the hill crossing fortified bridges, little moats, drawbridges, and, most fascinating of all, through 14 gates, each with its unique way to do in the enemy. Some gates have walls with spiked doors that descend from the ceiling, others have holes for hot oil, others inner rooms to capture the invader. It is lots of fun. As you near the summit there is a path leading off to an exquisite little chapel. Be sure to take the detour because the chapel is as pretty inside as it is out. Once you have conquered your castle, there is nothing of special interest—a small museum of arms, a few pictures, and a very nice courtyard—the fun is in the approach. There is a nice restaurant in the courtyard for lunch or a glass of wine.

DESTINATION IV　　　　KITZBÜHEL

There are many trains that pass through the Pörtschach station—watch for the one that will be marked to Salzburg. After boarding, settle back and relax: the scenery en route is sensational. The train follows the shoreline and then stops in the city of Villach before heading north.

9:38 am Leave Pörtschach by train
11:44 am Arrive Schwarzach/St. Veit

12:12 pm Leave Schwarzach/St. Veit by train
1:29 pm Arrive Kitzbühel

Schwarzach/St. Veit is a small station and the connection is easy. The train to Kitzbühel usually comes on the track next to the one where you arrive and will be marked to Innsbruck. Do not be concerned when you board the train and it seems you are heading back the way you just came—you are, but in only a short while the train changes direction and heads directly west toward Kitzbühel. The ride is lovely as the train follows a gentle valley bordered by low, tree-covered mountains. Before long you will see the lake, Zell am Zee. The train traces its shoreline before rushing on again through the wide valley. Soon the soft hills swell into enormous rocky summits of great beauty that herald the arrival of Kitzbühel.

Upon arrival in Kitzbühel take a taxi to your hotel. We recommend two hotels in Kitzbühel, the **Romantik Hotel Tennerhof**, a superb hotel idyllically located in the gentle hills just outside of town, and the **Hotel Strasshofer**, a small hotel in the center of town. See the hotel section for details on both of these.

Kitzbühel, a charming walled town, is a very popular tourist center both in summer and winter. It is the epitome of what one pictures when one thinks of the Tyrol—a colorful village whose painted buildings echo the past, charming little squares, inviting shops, walls surrounding the town, picturesque old gates, and mountains looming up from every view. Although this is a small town, there are a few sights to see such as the **Pfarrkirche** and the **Liebfrauenkirche**, two churches with lovely paintings to admire. But sightseeing is not the emphasis in Kitzbühel—instead, just relax and soak in the charm of the Tyrol. Try to linger here for several days: one day take the cable car up to the mountain peaks and meander for kilometers along well marked paths through some of the loveliest scenery in Austria.

DESTINATION V   FELDKIRCH

Note: Although this itinerary follows a route leading directly west to the scenic town of Feldkirch almost on the Swiss border, there are several excellent options for those who wish either to travel on to Germany or else to complete their circle and return to Salzburg. As an example, there is a train that leaves Kitzbühel about 9 am and arrives in Munich about 10:30 am. The return train trip to Salzburg takes about three hours. However, if you are heading into Switzerland, or have the time to extend your Austrian holiday, enjoy the beautiful train ride from Kitzbühel to Feldkirch. The train should have a dining car for you to enjoy a meal en route.

You can make a shorter connection time than shown below, but we indicate a schedule to allow time for sightseeing in Innsbruck.

9:29 am Leave Kitzbühel by train
10:35 am Arrive Innsbruck

2:39 pm Leave Innsbruck by train
4:51 pm Arrive Feldkirch

As the train leaves Kitzbühel the scenery is dazzling. Gigantic mountains soar into the sky, their jagged peaks scratching the clouds. The sullen grandeur of the mountains is intensified by the softness of the meadows in the foreground. It is so beautiful that you will be thankful you are on a train with no driving distractions. About an hour after leaving Kitzbühel the train makes a stop in Innsbruck. If you wish to do some sightseeing in Innsbruck, either check your suitcases directly through to Feldkirch or deposit them in the baggage room at the Innsbruck train station.

As the train approaches, **Innsbruck** looks like just another large city, but within a few minutes of the station there is a colorful town snuggled within medieval walls. In this inner heart of Innsbruck, you find many stunning old buildings, splendid churches, and a majestic central pedestrian square. To enjoy Innsbruck, walk around the charming city, have lunch in one of the enticing sidewalk cafés, and then take one of the later trains to Feldkirch. Note: If you want to overnight in Innsbruck, we recommend three hotels in the hotel section.

Feldkirch has not yet become "touristy." It is tiny, but reminiscent of Salzburg with its beautiful setting, maze of streets, and colorful old buildings. The mountains rise at the edge of town and, if you look up, you see a large castle commanding a rocky perch. Feldkirch still retains some of its old walls, old gates, and towers. The two main streets are lined with picturesque arcaded houses with oriel windows, turrets, and towers. Pretty shops stretch up and down the network of pedestrian streets, and outdoor cafés offer refreshments. This 13th-century town is truly a gem.

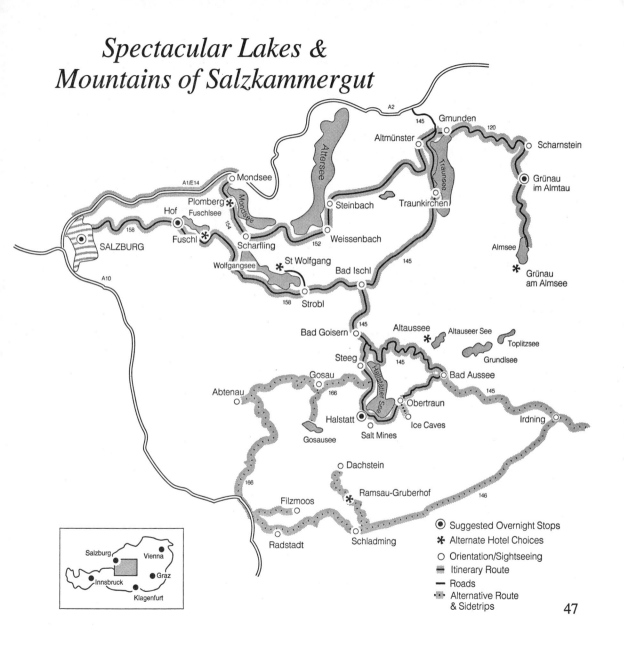

Spectacular Lakes &
Mountains of Salzkammergut

A2

145 Gmunden 120

Altmünster ○ Scharnstein

Attersee ○ Grünau
im Almtau

A1/E14 ○ Mondsee

Traunsee

Plomberg ✱ ○ Steinbach Traunkirchen

Hof Fuschlsee

Fuschl ✱ Scharfling 152 ○ Weissenbach Almsee

Wolfgangsee ○ St Wolfgang ✱ Grünau
am Almsee

SALZBURG

Wolfgangsee ✱ St Wolfgang ○ Bad Ischl 145

A10 158 ○ Strobl

145 Altaussee ○

Bad Goisern ○ ✱ Altauseer See Toplitzsee

Steeg ○ Grundlsee

Gosau ○ 145 Bad Aussee

Abtenau ○ 166 ○ Obertraun 145

Halstatt ◉ Ice Caves ○ Irdning

Gosausee ○ Salt Mines ○

○ Dachstein

166 Ramsau-Gruberhof 146

Filzmoos ✱

○ ◉ Suggested Overnight Stops

Radstadt ○ Schladming ✱ Alternate Hotel Choices

○ Orientation/Sightseeing

░ Itinerary Route

— Roads

░ Alternative Route
& Sidetrips

Salzburg ○ Vienna
○ Graz
Innsbruck ●
Klagenfurt ●

47

Spectacular Lakes & Mountains of Salzkammergut

The area close to Salzburg is called Salzkammergut, meaning "Land of the Salt Mines," a rather bland title for one of the most beautiful sections of Austria. Salt, a precious commodity, was responsible for Salzburg's early prominence and wealth, a wealth still visible in splendid palaces, stunning cathedrals, and magnificent castles. But none of these can compete with the splendor of nature—meadows of wildflowers painting pockets of vibrant color between dark-green forests, splendid lakes reflecting snowy mountain peaks in the early morning sunlight, small hamlets hiding behind swells of rolling hills, villages snuggled in little coves of gray-green lakes, gigantic mountains pushing their jagged, rocky peaks into the sky. This itinerary could be used as a reference for planning day trips from Salzburg. Another option would be to study this itinerary, choose one of the towns which sounds most intriguing and use it as a base. However, each destination suggested has its own special personality, so try to budget your time to linger in each area. Explore the ice caves, journey down into the salt mines, discover your own little lake, hike up into the mountains, and circle the lakes by ferry. Relax and soak in the spellbinding beauty of Austria.

ORIGINATING CITY   SALZBURG

This itinerary begins in Salzburg, a small city that is almost too perfect. It is like a stage setting with its maze of narrow streets, colorful medieval buildings, small squares, large plazas, and dramatic churches. The Old Town is squeezed in between the Salzach river and a rocky mountain on which there sits an enormous castle, once the residence of the powerful prince-archbishops of Salzburg. For sightseeing suggestions refer to the itinerary *Highlights of Austria by Train & Boat–or Car.*

DESTINATION I   GRÜNAU IM ALMTAL

Get an early start this morning so you can enjoy the scenery en route to your first destination. Leaving Salzburg, drive east for about 15 kilometers on the A1-E14 and watch for signs for the Mondsee exit. Just a few minutes south of the expressway, the Mondsee is the first of the lakes you explore on this itinerary. At the north tip of the lake is the town of **Mondsee** with its 17th-century church facing the village square. The beautiful baroque church with its twin steeples, each decorated with a matching clock, was used for the wedding scene in *The Sound of Music.* Drive up the road just behind the church and in a few minutes you will see signs for the outdoor museum **Mondseer Rauchhaus** (Smoking House) located on a small hill behind the church. Here you will find several old, very simple farmhouses that show the early Austrian way of life. The main building is reminiscent of early American frontier log cabins. The rooms are furnished with country antiques including a lovely cradle, interesting wooden hand-carved chairs, wonderful old beds, and wooden tables. The smoke that rose from the open fireplace into the attic loft was used for smoking meats. While in Mondsee sample their delicious Mondsee cheese, named for the lake and the town.

After brief sightseeing in the town of Mondsee, follow the road that hugs the west shore of the lake along Highway 154 (the signs will read "Saint Gilgen" and "Bad Ischl").

Continue south along the lake and in a few minutes the road splits. Follow the signs heading east to the Attersee, a few minutes' drive away. Upon reaching the lake follow the south shoreline for about 7 kilometers to Weissenbach and then continue north along the east rim of the lake toward Steinbach where a small sign directs you east to Altmünster. As the road climbs the hill, look back to see a gem of a small, onion-domed chapel which completes a "postcard-pretty" picture with the lake as a background. A 20-minute drive first climbs up through lush forest and then drops down the other side of the pass through small farms and meadows to the Traunsee.

When you reach the Traunsee turn north, tracing the lake. In a few minutes you arrive at

Schloss Ort, Gmunden

the old town of **Gmunden**. Visit the **Schloss Ort**, a tiny castle on a miniat᷉ the lake. Cross the bridge onto the island and wander around the pictur᷉ whose courtyard is surrounded by arcaded balconies. One side of the courtya᷉ pretty little chapel.

Gmunden makes a nice luncheon stop since there are many restaurants in the town. Before dining, check the ferry schedule at the pier so that you can linger over your lunch, leaving just enough time to board the wonderful old-fashioned ferry that circles the lake. (Usually there is a boat leaving about 1 pm for a three-hour trip.) If the day is nice, the boat ride is highly recommended since the Traunsee is an especially lovely lake— particularly the southern section where the heavily forested hills rise like walls of green from the water's edge.

After lunch and your "cruise," leave Gmunden following the small Highway 120 west for about 15 kilometers to Scharnstein where you turn south for about 7 kilometers to **Grünau im Almtal**. Drive through town and just after crossing the bridge look to your right and you will see the **Romantik Hotel Almtalhof**. This is an exceptionally delightful small hotel. Not only is the chalet-style hotel filled with rustic antiques, it is also filled with the warmth and caring of the Leithner family who own and manage this small inn. Their personal touch is everywhere. Frau Leithner is a cross-stitch artist and her handiwork is on pillows, door plaques, wall hangings, napkins, tablecloths, and little rugs. Herr Leithner is also an artist: he designed and built most of the wonderful rustic pine furniture in the bedrooms. The food, too, is very special, with most of the ingredients fresh from the garden or orchard.

The Romantik Hotel Almtalhof makes a perfect base for exploring the beautiful **Almtal Valley** and the **Cumberland Wildlife Park**. To begin your adventures, you do not have to go far. There is a delightful road south from Grünau im Almtal leading through a splendid forest: the prize at the end of the road is a small jewel of a lake, the **Almsee**. Here, nestled by the lake, is a charming small inn, the **Gasthof Deutsches**, which is also commended in the hotel section of our guide. It has a cheerful terrace restaurant where you might enjoy a snack. Afterwards, follow some tempting paths through the meadows that circle the lake.

DESTINATION II   HALLSTATT

When it is time to leave Grünau im Almtal, retrace your steps to Gmunden, and from there follow the road south along the west bank of the Traunsee for the short drive to Traunkirchen, situated on a small peninsula that gracefully extends into the lake. Then drive on to the south tip of the Traunsee where you leave the lake and continue south following the signs for Bad Ischl, a spa town made famous by Franz-Josef who spent holidays here with his family. The setting of the town is splendid. The Ischl and Traun rivers join in **Bad Ischl**, creating a loop of water around the spa which is still a popular health resort.

Stop to visit Franz-Josef's hunting lodge, Kaiservilla, located on the north bank of the Ischl (watch for the signs as you drive into town). Park your car and walk across a bridge to visit the lodge which is filled with hunting trophies. The house is not elaborate in design or decor, but the gardens are splendid. Continue south from Bad Ischl through the smaller spa town of Bad Goisern and a few minutes farther arrive at Steeg, the first town on the north end of the Hallstätter See.

Follow the road as it winds around the west side of the lake and continue a short distance on to the town of **Hallstatt**. You will not have a problem spotting your hotel, the **Gasthof Zauner**. As you stand in the main square of Hallstatt, with your back to the lake, you will see it peeking out from the far left corner of the plaza. In summertime the hotel balconies overflow with geraniums, making the hotel even easier to spot. The Gasthof Zauner is not a deluxe hotel, but it has great charm, warmth of welcome, and wonderful food.

Hallstatt

Of all the scenic places in Austria, none can outshine the amazingly picturesque small village of Hallstatt, whose quaint houses cling to the hillside as it rises steeply from the blue lake. Narrow alley-width streets twist their way up the hillside. A small church was built strategically near the edge of the lake, making a gorgeous picture as its pointed steeple reflects in the deep-blue waters. When the weather is calm, the mountains encircling the dark, still waters give a fjord-like beauty to this idyllic scene.

Hallstatt has a population of only about 500, but in spite of its size, there are many things to see. The stellar attraction is the setting itself—the town is built upon a shelf of land that drops down to the lake. The main square is at lake level, but the rest of the town climbs the hill with the houses built along streets that are staircases.

Hallstatt is Austria's oldest town: excavations show settlement here as far back as 400 B.C.. There are two museums in town, and one entry ticket is valid for both. The museums contain natural history exhibits and artifacts from the early salt-mining days. In addition to the museums there are two churches. A lovely one sits on the main square, but the more dramatic is the **Evang Church**, reached by a winding staircase from the center of town. Be sure to go inside to see the beautiful altarpiece painted in the 16th century and given to the church by a wealthy wine merchant.

Hallstatt is not only a very picturesque small lakeside town, it is also a wonderful base for interesting side trips. The obvious one is the ferry that departs from the pier to some of the other towns on the lake. This is fun to do, although the lake trips are short. Another trip, just a few kilometers from Hallstatt, is a must—the **Salt Mines**. For this excursion drive to the nearby town of Lahn where you will see signs to the funicular.

Park your car and take the funicular up the steep incline, where you find at the top a restaurant with a spectacular panorama of the lake and mountains. After a cup of coffee or some lunch, follow the signs to the salt mines. The path leads across a meadow and up a hill—about a ten-minute walk—to the main lounge where you buy a ticket and wait until your tour number is called. Then follow the guide into what looks like a locker room where pajama-like outfits are hanging according to sizes—small, medium, large. Here you put on loose scrub-suit-looking pants and tops over your clothing. After a few laughs you continue with your guide into the tunnel. The guide will probably not speak English, but if you have visited the mining museum in Hallstatt, you will certainly get the general idea of what is being said as you tag along with the group along a route which descends deeper and deeper into the earth.

Salt Mines, Hallstatt (Lahn)

You will not need an interpreter when you arrive at the gigantic wooden slide worn smooth as velvet over the years, one of those placed at strategic points to speed the miners' journey underground. Those still young at heart will love the ride, but for the less adventurous, a staircase parallels the slide to the bottom where you again follow the leader as you weave through a labyrinth of tunnels. (You will quickly see why you need your guide.) Before your adventure is over, you will have conquered another slide, seen an underground lake, had an audio-visual lecture on the caves (you probably will not understand a word), and walked for an hour. The tour ends dramatically. The group climbs up on a small train which consists of bench-like cars, then, once all are aboard, the brake is released and the train zips down the incline for about a kilometer and out again into the open air. A true adventure.

Another "must" from Hallstatt is a visit to the **Ice Caves,** or *Dachsteineishöhle.* To reach the caves follow the road to the south end of the lake towards the town of Obertraun. As you near the town, watch for the sign for the road which branches to the right to the Dachsteineishöhle. The name says it all—a hole with ice in the Dachstein mountains. But it is much more: even if caverns are not your "thing," give these a try—it is a real adventure.

Park in the designated car park by the gondola building, then buy a ticket and wait your turn. There are several choices for ticket purchase since the gondola climbs to various stages of the mountains for the convenience of skiers and hikers. You want the *Eishöhle* which will be well marked. When you reach the top, there is about a 20-minute hike up a trail to the ice caves. The walk is a bit strenuous but the path is well maintained and the views as you stop to catch your breath are glorious—you have a bird's eye view of the Hallstätter See. When you reach the entrance to the caves you must wait until the guide arrives—usually a handsome, athletic "outdoorsy" type. When the group is ready you follow the leader into the cavern. At first it does not seem anything special, just another enormous cave. Be patient though, because as the trail winds deeper into the earth, the walls of rock gradually become walls of ice. You enter a magic kingdom where you are surrounded by translucent, ever-changing mysterious forms of ice. To enhance the scene, at the most spectacular displays the guide turns on colored lights that fade, then brighten, then shade into rainbow colors.

Another suggested excursion from Hallstatt is a loop that takes you through some beautiful countryside south of Hallstatt. To do this, drive north for a few minutes, and then west for about 10 kilometers on 166 to the town of Gosau. Here a road branches to the south to the spectacularly lovely little lake, **Gosausee.** Although tiny, this lake is definitely worth a side trip. Rock walls rise straight up from the depths of the lake enclosing the dark-blue waters in a majestic embrace. The mighty peaks of the Dachstein mountains form a backdrop for this beautiful stage setting. Try to arrive at the lake before 9 am for two reasons—in early morning on a clear day the surface of the lake is like a mirror reflecting the mountains in all their glory, and in early morning the busloads of tourists have not yet arrived. Take a walk around the lake: there is a magnificent trail that takes about an hour to complete.

After visiting the lake, return to Gosau and follow the main road west for about 14 kilometers, watching as the road heads south, still marked 166. The road is narrow but the views are splendid as it follows a beautiful gorge then travels over a low pass for about 24 kilometers to Niedernfritz and then east to Radstadt. **Radstadt**, built in the 13th century by the archbishops of Radstadt, still maintains its ancient town walls and moats.

Schladming

From Radstadt continue east for about 20 kilometers to another medieval village, **Schladming**. During the Middle Ages silver and copper were both mined here.

The Dachstein massif rises impressively to the north of Schladming. Here is one of Austria's playgrounds for sports enthusiasts, both winter and summer. Lovely farms dot the lush green fields, mingling with newer chalets and hotels to care for the skiers. If time allows, take a loop north of the highway to the high **Ramsau am Dachstein** plateau. Wind up the mountain, watching for signs to **Gruberhof**, one of the small hamlets that cluster in the mountain meadows. Here you find **Zur Gruberstube**, one of the most idyllic hideaways you could ever dream of for lunch or a snack stop. This small, 18th-century farmhouse oozes charm, both inside and out. If the weather is nippy, you might want to eat in the cozy, antique-filled dining room. However, the favorite spot for guests to congregate is outside on the terrace, overlooking a stunning panorama of mountains and valleys. The food is simple and outstanding. As an added bonus, when the weather is agreeable, you can watch the colorful "birds" from the paraglider school in the adjacent meadow take flight. Note: Zur Gruberstube has one large apartment available for rent if you want to spend the night (see the hotel section for details).

After your side excursion to Ramsau, return to highway 146 and continue east for approximately 30 kilometers then turn north on 145 to complete your loop back to Hallstatt.

Zur Gruberstube and the Dachstein Massif, Ramsau

If you enjoy being out of doors, and if the weather is kind, there is another beautiful excursion from Hallstatt. From Hallstatt, follow the signs to Bad Aussee. About 5 kilometers east there is a string of lakes: a large lake, the **Grundlsee**, a medium-sized lake, the **Toplitzsee**, and a tiny lake, the **Kammersee**. All make wonderful targets for a long hike, with perhaps a picnic en route.

DESTINATION III   HOF BEI SALZBURG–FUSCHLSEE

When it's time to leave Hallstatt, head north to Bad Ischl, then turn west to Strobl. From Strobl it is only a few kilometers farther to the Wolfgangsee and a few kilometers more to the town of **Saint Wolfgang**, located on the northern shore. Saint Wolfgang is deserving of a visit although in season it is jammed with tourists. The **parish church**, though small, is splendidly embellished with beautiful works of art and deserves first notice. Next, you might want to have a snack on the lakefront deck of the **White Horse Inn** (of operatic fame). The ferry boat docks next to the hotel. Before leaving Saint Wolfgang, walk to the pier and board one of the boats which make a circle trip of the romantic lake. In Saint Wolfgang we recommend for accommodation the **Landhaus zu Appesbach**.

Saint Wolfgang

The hills rise so steeply beyond Saint Wolfgang that the road ends a short distance west of the village, so you must backtrack to the main highway and then continue along the south shore of the lake to the resort town of **Saint Gilgen**, a beautiful little village on the west shore of the Saint Wolfgangsee. The town has a delightful lakefront garden and also a picturesque medieval section encircling the main square dominated by a wonderful onion-domed church. Not only was Mozart's mother born in Saint Gilgen, his sister Nannerl lived here after she was married, so mementos of the Mozart family are everywhere.

At another lake nearby, the Fuschlsee, we recommend several hotels. The most luxurious, and truly memorable, is the **Schloss Fuschl** at Hof bei Salzburg which has a superb setting on a tiny finger of a peninsula that juts into the lake. If you budget is not quite up to the Schloss Fuschl, we also recommend two other places, the **Hotel Schützenhof**, a pretty small hotel right on the lake, and the **Jagdhof am Fuschlsee**, both at Fuschl am See and under the same ownership as the Schloss Fuschl.

Schloss Fuschl, Fuschlsee

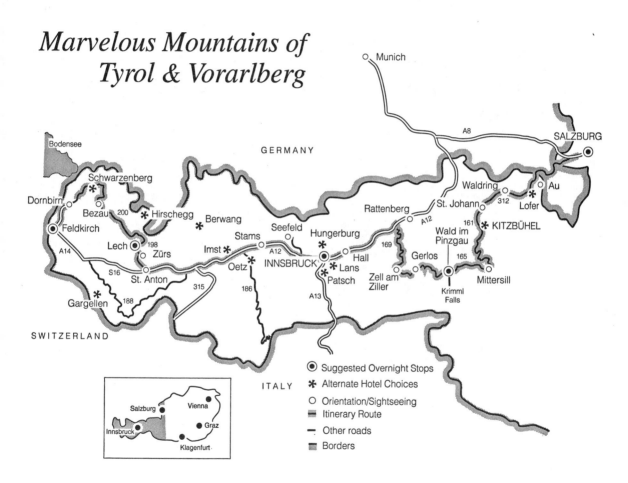

Marvelous Mountains of Tyrol & Vorarlberg

Munich

GERMANY

SALZBURG

A8

Bodensee

Schwarzenberg

Dornbirn

Bezau 200 ✱ Hirschegg

Feldkirch

Berwang

Waldring

Au

✱

Rattenberg

St. Johann

312 Lofer

Lech ✱ 198

A14

Zürs

Stams

Seefeld

Hungerburg

A12

161 ✱ KITZBÜHEL

Imst ✱

A12

Wald im
Pinzgau

S16

INNSBRUCK

Hall

169

Gerlos

165

St. Anton

Oetz

✱ Lans

315

186

Patsch

Zell am
Ziller

Mittersill

Gargellen

188

A13

Krimml
Falls

SWITZERLAND

ITALY

◉ Suggested Overnight Stops

✱ Alternate Hotel Choices

○ Orientation/Sightseeing

▥ Itinerary Route

— Other roads

▥ Borders

Salzburg

Vienna

Innsbruck

Graz

Klagenfurt

61

Marvelous Mountains of Tyrol & Vorarlberg

When one hears the word "Tyrol" wonderful visions dance in the mind—lush green fields with lazy cows munching grass, their huge bells ringing with the rhythm of each step, little boys with apple cheeks wearing leather shorts held up with jaunty suspenders, little girls with blond braids dressed in gay dirndls, picture-perfect villages with every small chalet decorated in geraniums, simple little churches standing on mountain ledges in isolated splendor, enormous farmhouse-barn combinations with plump down pillows dangling and airing from the windows, meadows of wildflowers stretching as far as the eye can see, powerful mountains rising like walls of granite into the sky. All this is true—and more.

Lofer

The province of Tyrol fills most of the narrow long western finger of Austria—a strip intersected by the Inn Valley, enclosed both to the north and south by spectacular mountains. The tip of the finger of western Austria is her smallest province, Vorarlberg. Combining the two provinces for an itinerary is logical, for together they make up the entire western section of the country, and although both are similar in their Alpine beauty, each has unique attributes to offer. This itinerary weaves across western Austria following one of the most scenic routes, suggesting sightseeing along the way, and staying in inns that capture the mood and beauty of the countryside.

ORIGINATING CITY   SALZBURG

After absorbing the splendors of Salzburg, a trip to the mountains of western Austria is like the icing on the cake. Salzburg is a beautiful little city, but always filled with people. The contrast of the countryside, where most of the sightseeing is of the grandeur of nature and where you will see many fewer fellow tourists, will make this itinerary all the more delightful. For sightseeing suggestions in Salzburg refer to the itinerary *Highlights of Austria by Train & Boat–or Car* beginning on page 29.

DESTINATION I   WALD IM PINZGAU

Leave Salzburg heading southwest in the direction of Innsbruck. Following the Saalach river, you traverse a short segment of Germany on road 21, but are soon back in Austria on the 312. As you re-enter Austria, the road winds along the river following a narrow canyon. Suddenly giant granite peaks soar behind conical-shaped hills—it is an incredibly beautiful scene.

Just before the town of **Lofer** (about a 14-kilometer drive from the border) watch for a small road leading off to the left to Au. Follow this road which circles to the left and in a couple of minutes you come to an elegant small pink chapel with a shingled roof and an onion dome, and with mountains rising in the background. This scene is captured on many Austrian postcards. Peek inside to see the pristine white walls accented by a lovely altar and lots of gold trim. Return to the main road and continue on to Lofer, an extremely picturesque old market town, with another stately onion-domed church on the main square. Stroll through town noting the many oriel windows and painted façades of some of the buildings. Be tempted by a cup of coffee and a pastry at one of the inns along the river that rushes through the town. Shopping is also an option as there are some excellent stores. You will find lovely sweaters (both for men and women) and an excellent selection of blouses and dirndls.

From Lofer continue west to **Waidring**, a small town with a tiny square sporting a delightful fountain and abounding with flowers and many chalet-style houses—some with roofs weighted down by stones.

A few kilometers beyond Waidring is another picturesque village, **Saint Johann**, surrounded by new condominiums announcing its popularity as both a summer and winter resort. Once through the maze of new construction, you will still find the heart of the old town with many of the houses covered in intricate, colorful paintings. Do not spend too much time, however, because the town is not as charming as Kitzbühel the next town on the itinerary.

From Saint Johann follow Highway 161 south watching for the signs to **Kitzbühel**. Stop in Kitzbühel to see the town whose beauty has made it a popular year-round destination for tourists from all over the world. Although no longer a tiny village, Kitzbühel still maintains the aura of a picture-perfect Austrian mountain hamlet. Drive through the gates of the medieval walls which still encircle the town, then park your car and explore the town on foot. A rigid building code has worked: the buildings all still reflect the glory of their past. Except for the many tourists, you will feel you have dropped into another era—a storybook setting of gaily painted old gabled houses whose windowboxes overflow with colorful flowers.

South from Kitzbühel along Highway 161 you pass through a wide valley of farmland and then head upward over a pass. After the summit, the road weaves downwards, hugging a mountainside that drops off sharply to the right and treats you to a magnificent bird's eye view of the splendid valley below. The first town you see as you enter the valley is **Mittersill**. If you like churches, you will find here not just one, but two baroque churches to explore. From Mittersill it is only about 30 kilometers west on 165 to **Wald im Pinzgau,** snuggled at the foot of the Hohe Tauern National Park. Continue past the town, which is to the left of the highway, and watch carefully for a small road on your right that weaves up the hill to a very special place to stay, the **Hotel Schöneben**. Its location in the lush Pinzgau Valley traced by the River Salzach is absolutely superb—an idyllic scene framed by soaring Alps. This small inn, whose heart dates back to 1604, is a Tyrolean treasure of rustic elegance.

Hotel Schöneben, Wald im Pinzgau

Just a few kilometers from the hotel, a small **museum** is housed in a wonderful old peasant's cottage. The museum has an excellent collection of gems that are mined in the mountains overlooking Wald. It is very interesting that only in this one small section of Austria have emeralds been discovered. The fame of these beautiful stones was such that it attracted buyers from as far away as Venice. (In fact, the highest peaks are called *Gross Venediger* and *Klein Venediger* in respect of these early Venetian tourists.) In addition to the rock collection, the museum also has many other exhibits including one on how honey was produced within very old beehives (of particular interest are two beehives whose doors open showing the bees very busy with their "honeywork").

Plan to linger in Wald. This is a wonderful place for hiking and exploring the countryside. Be sure to include a nearby attraction, one of the most famous sightseeing destinations in Austria, the **Krimml Falls**, the largest in Europe. As you leave the town of Wald, the road splits: the road to the right is the old mountain pass and the road to the left is a toll road. Take the road to the left marked to Gerlos and 7 kilometers outside Wald the falls are visible in the distance gushing from the mountains. A few minutes after spotting the Krimml Falls, you see a parking lot on the right side of the road.

From there it is about 20 minutes along a well marked path to the bottom of the waterfalls. There are lovely views along the way plus a couple of cafés should you need a little refreshment en route. There is a splendid view of the falls from below where they crash to the floor of the valley and join the river which flows on through the forest. If it is a lovely day, you might want to allocate three hours and climb the path that weaves up the mountain to higher vista points.

DESTINATION II   INNSBRUCK

When it is time to leave Wald, continue west on 165 toward Gerlos. The road splits and you can choose either the regular highway or a toll road to go over the pass. We suggest the toll road. Keep your stub because you will need it when you pass through the station at the other end. The road over the pass is beautiful. As you climb the mountain, the road makes a series of hairpin turns en route to the summit, then curves down the other side. As the road nears the next valley, you pass a small artificial lake on your left and then arrive at the famous high-mountain ski resort of Gerlos.

From Gerlos the road crosses an open valley and then twists down through the trees to an even lower valley and the town of **Zell am Ziller**. Once a gold-mining center, the town still retains remnants of its past glory with a lovely **parish church** and its most impressive dome painted by Franz-Anton Zeiller. Visit the church and then head north on Highway 169 for about 32 kilometers to the main Expressway A12.

Travel this expressway east for about five minutes to the joint exit for Kramsach and Rattenberg. When you leave the freeway follow the signs to **Rattenberg**. This is a picturesque medieval walled town that rose to prominence because of its valuable salt mines. These were exhausted in the early part of the 18th century, but now the town is famous for the production of fine glassware—a craft brought to Rattenberg many years ago by refugees from Czechoslovakia. The streets are lined with many shops selling all kinds of glass, most of which are finely engraved or etched. You can watch the craftsmen at work and have your name or initials carved while you wait. Prices are low and the shops will mail packages home tax free—a savings which more or less pays for the postage.

After your shopping expedition, return to the main Expressway A12 and head west following the signs to Innsbruck. Before reaching Innsbruck, make a stop in **Hall**, which in medieval times was one of the most important towns in the Tyrol due to the mining of that most precious commodity—salt.

Leaving Hall, it is a few minutes more to **Innsbruck**. If you want to stay out in the countryside, we recommend several lodging choices in the hills surrounding Innsbruck (see the hotel section). However, to enjoy Innsbruck to its fullest, it is fun to stay right in the heart of town. We suggest three places to stay in Innsbruck, the **Weisses Rössl** and

Goldenes Dachl, Innsbruck

the **Goldener Adler,** both beautifully located in the pedestrian-only section of the city, and the Schwarzer Adler, just a few minutes' walk away.

While meandering through the old town in Innsbruck, be sure to stop and admire the **Goldenes Dachl** (Little Golden Roof) which is an intricately carved balcony added to the Ducal Palace to commemorate the marriage of Maximilian I to Bianca Maria Sforza. Legend says that the gold roof of the balcony was commissioned by Duke "Friedrich the Penniless" to disprove the rumors of his poverty. This colorfully painted little balcony was used as a box by privileged royal guests to view in regal grandeur festivities taking place in the square below.

Another target should be the **Hofburg Palace,** built by Maria Theresa, where you can soak up the wealth and grandeur of the Hapsburg dynasty. Pause to admire the family portraits of Maria Theresa and her children.

When it is time to continue your journey, take the A12 and continue west following the River Inn. If you are a sports enthusiast, watch for a road and signs leading north a few kilometers beyond Innsbruck for **Seefeld,** a town familiar to all as the setting for the excitement generated by two Olympic games.

After visiting Seefeld, return to the main Expressway A12 and continue west. A few kilometers farther you come to the town of **Stams.** A stop in Stams is certainly worthwhile to visit the splendid 13th-century **Cistercian Abbey.** This abbey is most impressive and has two marvelous towers crowned by onion domes.

Return to the highway and continue west for about 55 kilometers following signs to Saint Anton and the Arlberg Pass. Park your car in Saint Anton and stroll along the main street which has been converted to a pedestrian mall with many fancy shops—clues to the international fame of **Saint Anton** as a jet-set ski resort. When you leave Saint Anton, do not return to the main highway, but instead follow the small road which winds along the mountain, first to the small town of Saint Christoph, and then twists its way north over the Flexenpass. Crossing the pass, the first town you come to is the ski resort of **Zürs.**

In winter this mountain paradise is a bustling ski resort, but in summer it is a barren little town standing almost deserted in a treeless high mountain valley. From Zürs the road drops farther into the valley and in a few minutes you arrive in **Lech,** an appealing village with lovely chalet-style hotels and shops lining both sides of a clear stream that rushes through the center of town. Because of its slightly lower elevation, Lech has many more trees and warmer weather than its sister ski resort of Zürs and therefore it is both a summer and winter resort—hiking is the sport in summer while in winter it is skiing. Hotel rates are lower in summer, but winter is a paradise too. If you are a skier, consider the fun of staying in Lech and taking the funicular to the top of the mountain to ski down for lunch at Zürs—the mountain lift systems all interconnect, making a giant spiderweb of skiing adventures and trails.

Lech

There are only a few very old buildings in the village, the most famous being a lovely small church dating from the 14th century. However, most of the new construction is consistent with the Alpine motif and blends harmoniously into the lovely valley. Lech's main reason for being today is tourism, and almost every place in town seems to offer rooms. We recommend three excellent accommodations to suit any budget—from the small, charming, **Pension Alpenland**, which is an outstanding value, to our super deluxe choices, the **Hotel Post** and the **Hotel Arlberg**, both lovely resort hotels (for details of these places to stay, look in the back of the guide in the hotel section).

DESTINATION IV   FELDKIRCH

On your way to Feldkirch we suggest you loop through the **Bregenzerwald,** a lovely region of the Vorarlberg. The name means "the forest near Bregenz," but it is much more. Bregenzerwald is an area of soft rolling hills, impressive walls of rocky cliffs, gentle pasture lands, the winding Bregenzer Ache river, lush forests, and, best of all, picturesque villages different from anything else found in Austria.

To reach the Bregenzerwald, continue north on 198 from Lech following the Lech river as it cuts a deep gorge far below the road. In spring, waterfalls leap from many of the cliffs and make inlets into the rushing river. As you near the town of Warth the canyon opens into a high mountain valley with meadows and farms. At Warth take road 200 heading west to Bezau. The road zigzags up and over the Hochtannberg Pass, where the landscape becomes wild and barren. There are some spectacular vistas, especially near the town of Nesslegg.

From Nesslegg the road drops quickly downward to the village of Schonbrunn, and from there you follow the valley floor, walled on both sides by lush green hills. Suddenly at Schoppernau the narrow valley spreads into an open meadow and you begin to see the colorful Bregenzerwald villages. Stop in the town of **Bezau**, one of the most typical of the small hamlets that dot the velvety meadows. Walk around the village: there are a few cute shops and restaurants, but the main attraction is the architecture and decor. Most of the buildings are shingled, most of a natural wood, but sometimes painted. Shutters, usually green, enclose the small paned windows. Look carefully at the windows—they make a beautiful picture. Peeking behind the windows are filmy white cotton curtains trimmed by an exquisite handmade border of lace. Accenting the white curtains are tied-back drapes, often in a country-French blue. Below the windows are flowerboxes of geraniums—the final perfect touch.

It is only about a five-minute drive from Bezau to **Schwarzenberg**, an even smaller hamlet well-known for dairy products. As you stroll around the village you will see a large cheese factory and in the early morning and evening the sound of cow bells ushers in the parade of cows which linger for a sip of cool water at the ancient fountain in the town square. The town is not only host to cows, but a great attraction to tourists because of the wonderful assortment of typical Bregenzerwald houses.

Leaving Schwarzenberg, follow the small back road through Bödele down into the town of Dornbirn. This is a very narrow road but the scenery is splendid. The road zigzags through the mountains and then drops down into Dornbirn. As you descend into the valley, the Bodensee (Lake Constance) appears in the distance. From Dornbirn, it is only a short drive to the main highway, A14, where you go south to **Feldkirch**, a jewel of a medieval town with an excellent place to stay, the **Hotel Alpenrose**.

From Feldkirch, it is just a few minutes' drive into Switzerland or Liechtenstein, or, heading north on A14, just a short drive to Germany.

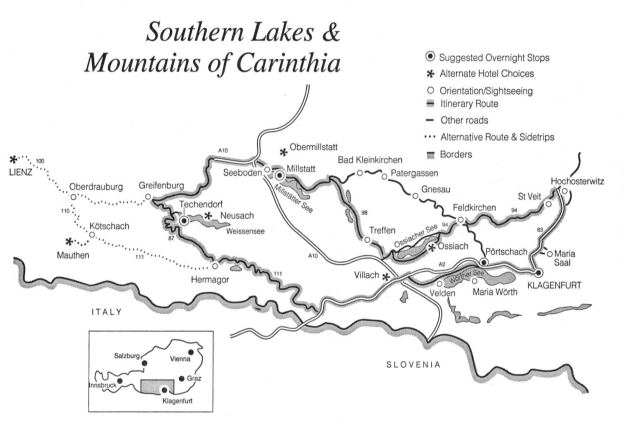

Southern Lakes &
Mountains of Carinthia

● Suggested Overnight Stops
✱ Alternate Hotel Choices
○ Orientation/Sightseeing
▬ Itinerary Route
— Other roads
••• Alternative Route & Sidetrips
▥ Borders

✱ 100
LIENZ

Oberdrauburg

Greifenburg

A10

Obermillstatt ✱

Seeboden ○ Millstatt ●

Bad Kleinkirchen

Patergassen ○

Hochosterwitz

110

Techendorf ● ✱ Neusach

Millstätter See

Gnesau

St Veit ○

Kötschach

Weissensee

98

Feldkirchen

94

Mauthen ✱

87

Treffen ○

Ossiacher See 94

83

111

Hermagor ○

111

A10

Ossiach ✱

Pörtschach ●

Maria Saal ●

Villach ✱

A2

Wörther See

KLAGENFURT ●

ITALY

Velden

Maria Wörth

SLOVENIA

Salzburg ●   Vienna ●

Innsbruck ●   ● Graz

Klagenfurt ●

73

Southern Lakes & Mountains of Carinthia

The lakes around Salzburg are gorgeous. Less well-known, but also of spectacular beauty, are the many lakes sprinkled among the mountains of southern Austria, in the province of Carinthia. Not only are these lakes lovely, but in summertime their waters warm to a comfortable temperature for swimming—sometimes an inviting 80 degrees Fahrenheit. Another plus, this patchwork of southern lakes is surrounded by majestic mountains including the mighty Dolomites whose jagged peaks form the border between Austria and Italy. The following itinerary leads you through the lake district. Although the total area is small and it would certainly be possible to base yourself in one resort and take side trips from there, each of the lakes has a special beauty and a unique character. If time allows, linger for a few days at each destination. If your time is limited, choose the lake and inn that seem most "you" and settle there. But whatever you do, try to incorporate this lovely part of Austria into your holiday.

Weissensee

Klagenfurt is easily reached by train, car, or airplane, making it a convenient starting point for a trip through the lake district of southern Austria. In addition to its geographic attributes, **Klagenfurt** merits admiration as an interesting medieval city. Like Vienna, the medieval walls of Klagenfurt were hauled down, and a circular ring road now encloses the heart of the old city where they once stood. At the center of this ring is the Neuer Platz, in the middle of which sits a statue of a marvelous old dragon, the emblem of the city. Perhaps there is some reality behind the legend of this fiery old dragon, for a skull of an ancient rhinoceros was found in the Klagenfurt area—perhaps at one time dragon-like creatures did roam these Lakes & mountains.

Klagenfurt

Sharing the central square with the dragon is a statue of Empress Maria Theresa. Surrounding the Neuer Platz is the Old Quarter with a handsome **parish church**, the old **Town Hall** (*Altes Rathaus*), the **House of the Golden Goose** (*Haus zur Goldenen Gans*), and an onion-domed **Landhaus**. If you arrive early in the day in Klagenfurt, stop briefly to enjoy the sights of the city and then continue to the first destination, Millstatt. However, if you arrive too late in the day to begin your journey, stay in the old city for the night so that you can browse through the shops and enjoy the sights of this once very important medieval town. Klagenfurt does not take long to see, and a one-night stay should be sufficient. Should you decide to overnight, a hotel suggestion is the **Romantik Hotel Musil**, which is well located, just a block from the central plaza. The decor is not outstanding, but there is an interior covered courtyard which is pleasant, and, best of all, a divine pastry shop.

DESTINATION I   MILLSTATT–OBERMILLSTATT

Leaving Klagenfurt, drive directly north on Highway 83 following signs to the airport. Five kilometers further on is **Maria Saal**, one of the most holy pilgrimage sites in Austria. Here in the 8th century, Bishop Modestus built a church dedicated to the Virgin Mary in which many people from the surrounding area were converted and baptized into Christianity. The original structure was rebuilt in the 15th century into a stunning twin-towered Gothic church. The town, located on a small hill just a short distance to the east of the highway, is well marked. As you drive to the town you cannot help spotting the large cathedral. The road winds up the hill and you park in a little square behind the church.

Return to the main Highway 83 and continue north for a few kilometers watching for the exit sign for **Hochosterwitz**, a wonderful old castle that looks exactly as a castle is supposed to look—majestically capping a very precipitous miniature mountain and displaying a hodgepodge of turrets, thick walls, and towers. This castle would certainly

Hochosterwitz

do justice to a fairy tale. The castle is visible long before you actually arrive, and is impossible to miss.

You cannot drive up to Hochosterwitz, so park your car, put on your sturdy shoes, and start your hike. It will take you about half an hour to walk to the castle, but the walk is really the essence of the castle and a sightseeing excursion in its own right. Ascending the hill, you pass through a succession of 14 gates designed by the most famous castle-fortification architect of the Middle Ages thanks to whom, because of his skill, the castle was never conquered.

You will soon see why this stronghold was never conquered. Each gate has its own unique brand of protection—one has holes through which hot oil was poured upon the invader, another has a moat, another a drawbridge, another hidden spikes, another fire-torch slots, and on and on. If the enemy was clever enough to conquer one gate, he was sure to be defeated before the final entrance. Just as you draw close to the top, a path leads off to a beautiful little chapel on a ledge overlooking the valley far below. Take the time to walk over to it. Not only is the view lovely, but the church interior is splendid in its combination of simple white walls and ornate gold altar. Upon reaching the summit, you will find a small museum, a central courtyard, a nice restaurant, and magnificent views.

From Hochosterwitz castle, return to the main highway and continue north for a few kilometers following the signs to **Saint Veit**, the medieval capital of Carinthia. As you approach the town you will notice the ruins of many medieval castles which at one time guarded this strategic route to Vienna. Upon reaching Saint Veit, follow Highway 94 west for about 23 kilometers to **Feldkirchen**, at one time an important medieval town belonging to the bishops of Bamberg. There you find a lovely old parish church and some picturesque houses.

Continue west on the 94 in the direction of Villach and after about 7 kilometers you come to the Ossiacher See. If you have time, take a short detour on the road to the south side of the lake to the tiny town of **Ossiach**. This is one of the few picturesque villages along this pretty lake that hosts mostly camping sites. Ossiach is a good place to have lunch and visit the **Benedictine Abbey**. Note: Part of the Benedictine Abbey is also open as **Stiftshotel Ossiach**—see our listing in the hotel section. After seeing Ossiach, return to the 94 and continue west in the direction of Villach. Just after the road leaves the lake (before you come to the freeway), watch carefully for 98 where you turn right (north) on the back road to the Millstätter See.

About 4 kilometers after the turnoff onto 98 (soon after passing Treffen), take a small road to your right, signposted to Winklern and **Elli Riechl's Puppenwelt**. Elli Riechl, who was born in Villach in 1902, always wanted a "little house in the mountains." When she became a widow at the age of 28, she fulfilled her dream and moved to a small farmhouse in the country. She loved being out of doors and took long walks where she became friends with all the local families and adored all their children. Elli began to make dolls based on the people in the valley, concentrating especially on young children.

Elli Riechl's Puppenwelt

Elli Riechl's passion for dolls continued until she died in 1977. A small farmhouse next to her workshop has been converted into a museum, beautifully displaying in glass cases over 600 examples of her work. Each of the small dolls is a masterpiece, beautifully crafted and dressed to perfection with clothes all sewn by Elli. Do not pass up this museum—even if you aren't much interested in dolls, this exhibition is enchanting. I promise you will come away smiling. The whimsical, happy children and adults depicted are absolutely irresistible. The museum is open from April 1 to May 31 and from

Hubertus Schlössl, Millstatt-Millstätter See

September 15 to October 15 from 9 am to noon; and from June 1 to September 15 from 9 am to noon, and 2 to 6 pm, tel: (04248) 2395.

After visiting the doll museum, continue north on 98 following signs to the **Millstätter See.** The road hugs the hillside above the water and you soon come to the most picturesque town along the lake, **Millstatt.** We recommend **Die Forelle Hotel, Hotel Post** and **Hubertus Schlössl** in Millstatt. However, one of our favorites, the charming **Hotel Alpenrose,** is not located in town, but nearby in the town of **Obermillstatt** which, as you might guess from the name, is a tiny village located high in the hills above Millstatt. All of our recommendations are described in detail in the hotel section at the back of the guide.

The old part of Millstatt is snuggled on the incline rising from the lake. Here you can visit the abbey which dates back to the 11th century. However, most tourists head for the lake where a promenade lined with hotels, restaurants, and small parks traces the water's edge. Boats are available for rent, but most fun of all is to walk down to the pier and take a relaxing excursion on one of the ferries that circle the lake.

When it's time to leave, our favorite lake in Austria awaits you. Follow 98 west along the north shore of the **Millstätter** See to the town of Seeboden and from there take the expressway heading west. Do not get too settled because you stay on the freeway for only a few minutes before leaving it to follow Highway 100 (also called E66) which will be marked to Lienz. The road follows the beautiful River Drau for about 20 kilometers to the town of Greifenburg where you leave the main highway and turn south following signs to the Weissensee. This is a spectacularly beautiful drive: the road curves up through beautiful green meadows and over a small pass to a high Alpine lake, the Weissensee. We have two hotel suggestions at the Weissensee. If you choose the **Gralhof Pension** continue along the road that follows the north edge of the lake to Neusach and you will see the hotel on the left side of the road across from the lake. If you choose the **Haus am See** turn right and in Techendorf cross the bridge that cuts across a narrow part of the lake. If you are staying at the lovely Haus am See, you can find it easily—it is to your left after the bridge—the only hotel directly on the lake.

The **Weissensee** is still "country"—the relatively few hotels are basically converted farmhouses nestled along the lake. Except for a small village at the end of the lake, the entire eastern half of the Weissensee is a nature preserve—off limits to any commercial development. Ferries circle the lake, but they are mostly to drop off passengers who want to hike along the beautiful path which completely encircles the pristine water. The lake is an incredible emerald-green color and in the early morning and late evening mirrors the steep green hills that rise precipitously along its eastern half in a fjord-like beauty. The western half of the lake is surrounded by more gentle hills that melt down into green lawns extending to the shoreline. There is no beach, but lounge chairs dot the grass and piers extend through the reeds into the water. The activities along the Weissensee are simple—no great sights to see, just the splendor of nature at its finest. Linger here and enjoy long walks, fishing, swimming, and boating.

You might never want to leave your oasis of tranquillity, but if the mood for sightseeing moves you to action, you can make a circle excursion to visit the old town of Lienz. To really enjoy this outing you should allow most of the day. First leave the Weissensee and retrace the road east down into the beautiful Drau Valley. At Greifenburg take the main highway west to Lienz. On approach, the town looks like a modern, uninteresting city. Cross the river and park at the car park near the center of the town, then walk into the heart of **Lienz** and you will be well rewarded. Although war destroyed much of the town's periphery, the core has been restored to its former picturesque self. A pedestrian mall is framed by colorful buildings. There are many cafés in the square—a great suggestion for lunch would be the outdoor restaurant of the **Romantik Hotel Traube**. After lunch and exploring the old town, visit **Bruck Castle** which sits on a hill above the city. This 16th-century castle, formerly belonging to the Counts of Gorz, has a museum with artifacts discovered in nearby excavations of Roman settlements, Austrian folklore and handicraft displays, and paintings by Tyrolean artists. From the castle you can look down into the city of Lienz and appreciate its lovely setting with mountains rising almost at the edge of the town.

From Lienz, return east along Highway 100 for approximately 15 kilometers to Oberdrauburg where a small road heads south and makes a series of criss-crosses as it climbs over the mountains before dropping down the other side into the next valley to the town of **Kötschach**. Just beyond Kötschach in **Mauthen**, we recommend the **Landhaus Kellerwand**. From here take the Highway 111 east following the Gail river. It is a beautiful drive made all the more rewarding by glimpses to the south of the fabulous jagged peaks of the mighty Dolomites marking the border with Italy. When you reach the town of Hermagor, turn north again and complete your circle back to the Weissensee.

When it is time for you to end your lake interlude, you have several options. You can head north and over the famous **Grossglockner Pass** into Salzburg, you can drive south and be in Italy in less than an hour, or you can complete your circle by returning to Klagenfurt. If time allows one more lake interlude, retrace the highway west along the Weissensee through the town of Techendorf and watch for the signs for Highway 87 going south toward Hermagor. At Hermagor, follow Highway 111 east toward Villach.

A few kilometers before Villach, the road becomes an expressway that bypasses Villach on its way toward Velden. Although it requires a slight detour from the freeway, **Villach** is an interesting city for a short visit. It will be easy to find the center of the **Old Quarter**—definitely the most interesting section. Just follow the church spire and you will come to the River Drau which makes a loop outlining the ancient part of town. In the center of town on the main square is a dramatic church whose steeple soars over 90 meters into the sky. Nearby are many picturesque old houses, little shops hiding in alley-like streets, and a 16th-century Rathaus. Just a few steps from the church is the **Romantik Hotel Post**, an excellent choice for a luncheon stop with its gourmet restaurant. Also of interest, in the Schiller Park is a huge relief map of Carinthia: this is especially fascinating because it is fun to mark the mountains and lakes you have been exploring.

Leaving Villach, return to the Expressway A2 and continue east following the signs to Velden, the popular resort and gambling center on the Wörther See. From Velden skirt the lake along the northern shore for the short drive to **Pörtschach**.

We offer two excellent hotel recommendations for Pörtschach. Just before entering the town, on the western fringe, you will see a road heading south across the railroad tracks and a sign pointing to the right along a small lane to the **Schloss Seefels**, a fancy yet tasteful lakefront resort—a superb hotel where you can relax in utter luxury. Farther along, in the town of Pörtschach, we recommend another castle, the lovely **Schloss**

Leonstein. Both hotels are very popular since many Austrians vacation at the Wörther See because it is one of the warmest of the lakes in Carinthia. An added bonus is the magnificent scenery as mountains rise in mighty splendor to the south, forming the border with Italy.

While in Pörtschach you can enjoy tennis, swimming, boating, shopping, and hiking. But one excursion you must not miss is taking the ferry that circles the lake. Be sure to get off to explore the picturesque village of **Maria Wörth** which clings to a tiny peninsula jutting out into the lake on its south side.

When it is time to end your holiday, it is only a few minutes to Klagenfurt. From there you can continue your journey by driving north to Salzburg or Vienna, flying to your next destination, or boarding one of the many express trains departing for another chapter of exciting places.

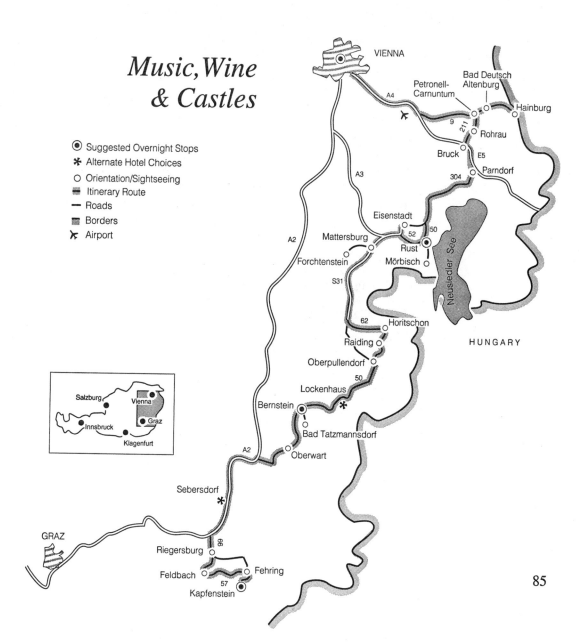

Music, Wine & Castles

Legend:
- ◉ Suggested Overnight Stops
- ✳ Alternate Hotel Choices
- ○ Orientation/Sightseeing
- ▦ Itinerary Route
- — Roads
- ▦ Borders
- ✈ Airport

VIENNA

Bad Deutsch Altenburg

Petronell-Carnuntum

Hainburg

Rohrau

Bruck

Parndorf

E5

304

A4

9

211

A3

Eisenstadt

52 50

Mattersburg

Rust

Forchtenstein

Mörbisch

Neusiedler See

A2

S31

62

Horitschon

Raiding

HUNGARY

Oberpullendorf

Lockenhaus

50

Bernstein

✳

Bad Tatzmannsdorf

A2

Oberwart

Sebersdorf

✳

GRAZ

Riegersburg

66

Feldbach

Fehring

57

Kapfenstein

Salzburg

Vienna

Innsbruck

Graz

Klagenfurt

Music, Wine, & Castles

This itinerary begins in Vienna, the city of music, and then goes south, tracing the eastern border of Austria. Most of the trip takes place in Burgenland, which literally means "land of castles." The name is appropriate: look closely and you will spot on almost every strategic mountaintop a castle or the ruins of a once-mighty fortress. The castles were a necessity, a defense against the fierce invaders from the Ottoman Empire whose dreaded warriors constantly passed through on their way to Vienna. Two of the suggested places to stay on this itinerary are castles that have been converted into hotels. Also stops are made en route at castles that are now open to the public as museums where you can relive again this fascinating, turbulent period of Austria's history.

Castles are not all that Burgenland has to offer: here you can sample some of Austria's finest wines (about one-third of the country's production comes from this area—the grapes are mostly grown around the mysterious Neusiedler See whose water occasionally simply disappears). In addition to castles and wine, Burgenland is famous as being Austria's cradle of music—some of Austria's finest musicians were born here. So, if you like castles, music, wine, and "off-the-tourist-track" adventures, follow this itinerary for a very special treat.

ORIGINATING CITY VIENNA

Vienna is a logical starting point for this itinerary since the boundary of Burgenland begins only a short drive from the city limits. For sightseeing suggestions refer to the itinerary *Highlights of Austria by Train & Boat–or Car*. While in Vienna soak in as much history as you can. There are superb bookstores here with a tantalizing selection of books written in English. Browse through them and buy a few—especially those dealing with the history of Austria. It will make this itinerary "come alive" as you later wander through Roman encampments, visit castles filled with weapons used against the invading Turks, and explore palaces owned by the wealthy Esterhazy family whose power rivaled that of the emperor. Also buy a book on the music of Austria: an especially good one is Richard Rickett's *Music and Musicians in Vienna*. As you later follow the trail of Haydn and Liszt (both sons of Burgenland) you almost hear the haunting melodies of their music when you visit their homes.

Absorb as much history as you can from the tour guides who take you through the Hofburg Palace. Ask about how Maria Theresa wrested power from the princes whose small kingdoms in Burgenland almost rivaled her own. On this itinerary you will be visiting some of the castles that belonged to her adversaries. Also while in Vienna, attend as many musical performances as you can, since you will be traveling through the province where many of Austria's great musicians were born. One of these was Haydn, who attributed the originality of his compositions to the fact that for so many years he was isolated in Burgenland where he could not copy the popular musical trends.

While in Vienna there are excellent hotel choices. Read the hotel section in the back of this guide to see which appeals most to your style and budget. Try to plan well in advance since Vienna is a very popular tourist destination and hotel space is always at a premium.

DESTINATION I   RUST

Leaving Vienna, take the Expressway A4, which follows the Danube Valley east. It is an easy route to find—just follow the Airport signs. The expressway ends, but a good road continues on toward the Hungarian border. About 24 kilometers beyond the airport you will come to **Petronell-Carnuntum** where signs on both sides of the road indicate footpaths to Roman ruins. There is now only a hint at what was once a stronghold of the Roman power in Austria: only a couple of amphitheaters located in open meadows, some ruins of Roman houses, and a lonely stone gate remain. (To see what was found in the excavations, continue on a few kilometers farther to the town of **Bad Deutsch–Altenburg** where most of the artifacts are displayed.) Although the excavation site is not dramatic, the Romans played such an important role in Austria's history that it is good to soak in a bit of the mood—and besides, the walk through the fields to the amphitheaters is very pleasant. A few kilometers farther east, almost on the border of the Czech Republic, is the medieval walled city of **Hainburg**. Although not an especially beautiful medieval city, Hainburg was very important due its strategic location and many famous battles were fought here. (Note: If you get a late start from Vienna, skip the Roman ruins and Hainburg, and begin the more important sightseeing as continues below.)

Leaving Hainburg, retrace your drive and return west along the Danube for about 8 kilometers, returning to Bad Deutsch–Altenburg where you take highway 211 south. In a few minutes you will arrive in **Rohrau**. Amazingly, this simple town was the birthplace of two musical geniuses, Franz Josef (1732–1809) and Michael Haydn (1737–1806). Just before you enter the town, watch on the left side of the road for the small whitewashed thatched cottage where Haydn (one of a family of 12 children) was born. **Haydn's birthplace** is now a small museum with just a few rooms. Of special interest are the many pictures of his fellow musicians.

Just beyond Haydn's birthplace, you will see on the right side of the road the large **Harrach Palace** dramatically surrounded by superb gardens. This estate ties in with Haydn's life as his mother was a cook for the wealthy Harrach family who were, and still are, the owners of this castle. But far more than the fact that Haydn's mother worked here, the castle is worth a stop because now it also houses one of the finest private art collections in Austria, the **Harrach Gallery**. Park your car and walk into the courtyard to buy your ticket to the museum. More than 200 paintings representing artists from all over the world are elegantly displayed in light, airy rooms. Do not miss a long corridor whose walls are lined with huge murals depicting famous Austrian battles: it is fascinating to see the battle formations and the homey touches such as women cooking the meals, children frolicking just behind the field of battle, and dogs following their masters. Note especially the dress and weapons—you will be seeing the real thing a little later on in this itinerary at Forchtenstein castle.

Continue south from Rohrau on 211 for a short way and you come to the A4. Take this south for about 5 kilometers (in the direction of Parndorf) and then go east on highway 304 in the direction of Eisenstadt and then south on highway 50. In a few minutes you will see ahead of you the Neusiedler See. Some of Austria's finest wines are grown in the fertile marshy lowlands stretching around the lake.

The **Neusiedler See** is intriguing. About once a century there is NO lake—it simply disappears. And then, for no apparent reason, it comes back again. There are almost no tributaries into the lake—the water seems to blossom forth from underwater springs. Another strange occurrence is that sometimes the lake shifts, rather like a tilting cup of water. When this takes place, land is quickly claimed, but before the arguments of possession are solved, the water usually shifts again and the land is recaptured by the mischievous lake. In spite of its naughty nature, the lake is fascinating: so shallow that a man can usually stand and keep his head above water at the deepest part, and so encumbered with reeds that long piers must extend out from the shore for access. Its very nature welcomes birds, and this is a paradise for the bird watcher—more than 250 species of birds, protected by law, make this their home.

As you drive south on 50, watch for a small road to the left, signposted to **Rust,** a charming village with picturesque old houses, many still with thatched roofs. Park your car in the center of town and wander around. Look carefully and you will see storks proudly perched on their rooftop nests. If you are lucky, you might even see a baby stork noisily asking for dinner. In addition to having quaint architecture and roofs decorated with storks, Rust also produces some of Austria's loveliest wines.

On the little streets leading off Rust's central square, you will frequently see evergreen branches tied above arcaded doorways, indicating a simple wine tavern within, where the owner serves his own wine. Step into the inner courtyard and sit down at one of the wooden tables for a bite to eat and a sample of the famous Rust wine. See if you agree with the Hungarian prince who was so fond of its wine that he gave Rust the stamp of royalty.

In a lovely 16th-century whitewashed building facing the main market square is one of Rust's most charming small restaurants—the **Rusterhof.** This is also our choice for a place to stay since above the restaurant are four prettily decorated guestrooms. Actually, the accommodations are more than "just" rooms—they are spacious one- or two-bedroom suites, each with cooking facilities. The Rusterhof makes a great base for exploring this wondrous region of Austria.

Once you settle into your hotel, drive a few kilometers farther south along the lake to **Mörbisch,** another wine town. Mörbisch is not quite as colorful as Rust, but is picturesque with many little lanes spanned by arcades that connect gaily painted houses.

DESTINATION II   BERNSTEIN

From Rust, head directly west on 52 to **Eisenstadt.** Eisenstadt is where Haydn lived for 30 years and brims with mementos of his musical genius. Continue straight into town and stay on the same street until you come to the **Schloss Esterhazy** (if you cannot find a place to park, there is a parking garage across from the palace). The powerful princes of Esterhazy, who incidentally claimed descent from Attila the Hun, were an immensely wealthy, powerful family in Burgenland and Hungary, their holdings rivaling those of the emperor, and at times their wealth surpassed his. It was a popular concept for wealthy nobles to have their own court musician, and Haydn was hired to lead the musical life at Schloss Esterhazy.

You must not miss the imposing Schloss Esterhazy: it is well worth a leisurely visit. Check with the tourist office before you leave home to try, if at all possible, to coincide your sightseeing with one of the concerts that are regularly performed here. If you miss a concert, another option is to time your visit with a short daytime musical performance. On a regularly scheduled basis, a group of musicians, dressed as they would have been in Haydn's day, play chamber music. This is outstanding—if your timing coincides with this event, do not miss it.

Take the tour of the castle itself which has recently been restored to its original grandeur. Buy a small pamphlet in English at the ticket desk so that you can appreciate what you see. There are excellent pieces of art, plus an ever-changing exhibition. When we last visited in 1995, there was an incredible display of personal belongings loaned to the museum by the Esterhazy family. Most memorable was a dining table exquisitely set with fantastic china, linens, and silver—as it would have been for a party given by the prince.

You will see several of the rooms where Haydn worked, including the highlight of the tour, the Haydn-Saal, a huge concert hall decorated with 18th-century frescoes. It was here that Haydn entertained the Esterhazy family and their friends almost every evening, usually with his own masterful compositions. The family constantly desired new pieces, which motivated Haydn to compose a stream of superb music. In fact, he must have never had a moment to relax since new compositions were expected from him to celebrate every birthday and other special occasion. Haydn attributed the originality of his music to his isolation in Eisenstadt where he could not copy the stilted music so popular in Vienna.

Either before or after the tour of the castle, take the short walk to **Haydn's home** (only about a block away). As you face the castle, the street where Haydn lived runs along the right side of the castle grounds. Follow this street and you will find his small house on the left side of the road, 21 Haydngasse, marked with a plaque. There is an appealing small courtyard but the house is not grand. Inside, the rooms are simple—mostly showing interesting photographs both of Haydn and his musical contemporaries. Near the piano a tape plays some of Haydn's delightful compositions. It is almost like magic—you feel he has returned and is playing especially for you.

Plan to eat lunch in Eisenstadt. The town has recently undergone extensive renovation and the plaza in front of the castle stretches out to an inviting pedestrian-only street with many restaurants and shops.

Leaving Eisenstadt, follow Highway S31 south watching for the town of Mattersburg, at which point you head west for a few kilometers to Forchtenstein Castle. You should not get lost because not only is the castle well signposted, it can also be seen from far away, dominating the top of a hill.

The approach road to **Forchtenstein Castle** twists up the mountain to the car park at the summit. The restaurant on the cliff next to the castle has a stunning view of the valley. The castle, originally built by the powerful Mattersburg family and then later rebuilt by the Esterhazies, was a key defense against the terrible Turks.

Forchtenstein Castle is still in fabulous condition and the castle tour is particularly interesting. In the museum you see the original equipment used by the Esterhazy army. This is a dazzling display—the largest private collection of armor in Europe. Even the Tower of London with its enormous military museum is not much more impressive. In some ways, the museum of Forchtenstein is even more interesting because it is more personalized.

Forchtenstein Castle, Mattersburg

You walk through enormous rooms where the equipment was kept—one complete room of helmets, another of spears, another of saddlebags. What a dramatic reminder of the power, wealth, and splendor of the Austrian nobility! The armory is not all there is to see, however. The kitchen is also very interesting with its giant spit over an open fire—seemingly large enough to roast meat for an army, which it probably did. In the

Music, Wine, & Castles

courtyard there is a well over 120 meters deep which was dug by some of the less fortunate Turks who were captured and had to work as slaves. Also on display are other mementos of the battles with the Turks: you will see many captured weapons and, most interesting of all, a wonderful Turkish tent, probably used by the commanding officer. In one of the corridors of the castle is an assortment of elaborate coaches and sleighs used by the Esterhazy family. All in all, a wonderful museum.

Leaving Forchtenstein Castle, return east to the main Highway S31 and continue south for about 15 kilometers to Weppersdorf then take 62 east for about 5 kilometers. At Horitschon turn south, following signs to **Raiding**, the birthplace of another musical genius, Franz Liszt. **Liszt's birthplace** is now a museum, the walls covered with musical mementos and photographs. It is interesting to see the photographs of many of Austria's musical masters, many of whose lives were interwoven. In the lobby is a small shop where you can purchase literature and musical tapes.

After a visit to Liszt's birthplace, return to highway 31 (which becomes highway 50 at Oberpulldorf) and continue on to your destination for the night, **Bernstein**. As you drive through town watch for a sign on the right side of the road leading up the hill to your hotel, **Burg Bernstein**. When the castle was transformed into a hotel, the original furniture was retained and because of this, the rooms vary tremendously. You might find yourself in a giant room with a bathtub tucked into the corner behind elegant drapes or a formally splendid room with severe ancestors peering at you from their frames of gold. Do not expect spiffy decorator touches: this castle is authentic and the furniture speaks its own message of bygone days—no cute touches are needed to set the mood. The dining room is outstanding—a large room with a lavishly detailed baroque ceiling and frescoes ornamenting the lovely alcoved windows. Burg Bernstein makes a good hub for exploring the many castles in the area.

As you leave Bernstein continue south along Highway 50. In a few kilometers you will come to the popular health spa of **Bad Tatzmannsdorf**. The town is not very interesting and quite crowded with tourists "taking the waters," but there is a splendid park in the center of town that you might want to see.

Driving south from Bad Tatzmannsdorf on Highway 50, you soon come to Oberwart. Five kilometers beyond Oberwart, turn right (west) on a small road that leads to the expressway A2. In 7 kilometers you hit the A2, which you take south in the direction of Graz. In about 28 kilometers you come to a turnoff to 66, which you take south toward Feldbach. From the junction, it is about 13 kilometers until you reach **Riegersburg** where you will see high above the town, to the right of the road, the sensational **Riegersburg Castle**. Park your car in town at one of the designated parking places and walk up the path to the castle. Be forewarned: it is at least a half-hour's hike. But if you are not in a hurry, the walk is part of the fun. When you finally reach the top, there is a restaurant where you can sit outside and enjoy the stunning panorama from your perch high in the sky.

You need to join a tour to visit the castle. The interior is not spectacular—it is the combination of the incredible setting, the views, and the structure of the castle that makes a trip here worthwhile. Note: As you climb up the path to the castle, before you reach the summit, there is a place to the right where falconry demonstrations are given. If this interests you, ask the tourist office in advance for the schedule.

After Riegersburg, continue south on 66 for approximately 9 kilometers. Just before you come to the town of Feldbach, 66 makes a junction with 68. Turn left (east) here and 4 kilometers later take highway 57 east to Fehring. When you come to Fehring, head south for about 7 kilometers to your destination, Kapfenstein. This region of Austria is glorious and Schloss Kapfenstein is the perfect site to capture its tranquil, unspoilt perfection.

Schloss Kapfenstein, Kapfenstein

As you approach **Kapfenstein**, the castle crowns a hill to the left of the road. Take the small road to the left that winds up through fields of vineyards, past a picture-perfect small yellow church, and on to the 12th-century **Schloss Kapfenstein.** You will get a hint of the gorgeous views as you approach the castle, but the splendid panorama only comes into sight when you reach the summit. The hotel is bounded by a romantic wide terrace and intimate little gardens with breathtaking views. Looking to the left you see Hungary, looking to the right you see Slovenia. Many of the well furnished bedrooms also afford beautiful vistas. Plan to end your holiday with a leisurely sojourn at the Schloss Kapfenstein. It is truly a very special place—one of our favorites. It is a simple hotel, but one with great heart. Apart from the stunning views, it also has comfortable accommodations, excellent food, outstanding wines (produced in the castle's own vineyards), and, best of all, genuine warmth of welcome from all the Winkler family.

The Schloss Kapfenstein makes a most fitting conclusion to the "Wine" portion of this itinerary since from the castle you can venture out each day to explore the vineyards in the region. The Winklers' son, Georg, and his wife, Margot, oversee the family's wine production. They will not only show you their own winery and introduce you to their own fine wines, but will gladly share with you other vineyards and towns to visit in the area.

Hotels

The Romantik Hotel Böglerhof is a refined, sophisticated resort beautifully situated in a picturesque Alpine village (claimed to be one of the prettiest in Austria) tucked high in the Alpbach Valley. Although the hotel offers all the amenities of a fancy hotel (indoor and outdoor pools, tennis, sauna, children's playroom, conference rooms, several dining rooms), it still maintains the warmth and charm of a small hotel. The property has been in the same family for three generations—Karin Duftner's father acquired the 15th-century farmhouse (which at the time was in sad disrepair) in 1933. Although it has been modernized and greatly expanded over the years, Karin and Johannes Duftner have taken great care to main the authentic ambiance of a Tyrolean home with wooden balconies draped in the summer with exuberant displays of pink and red geraniums. The mood is set as you enter into the spacious lobby, filled with antiques and large bouquets of freshly cut flowers. In addition to the attractive dining room for guests who are on a half-pension meal plan, there is a fabulous stüble-style dining room with the original paneled walls and ceiling gleaming with the patina of age. The guestrooms are mostly of built-in, blond-pine furniture—a modern interpretation of the Tyrolean style. The rooms vary from standard double rooms to two-bedroom suites that are perfect for families.

ROMANTIK HOTEL BÖGLERHOF
Owners: Karin & Johannes Duftner
6236 Alpbach, Tyrol, Austria
Tel: (05336) 52.27 Fax: (05336) 52.27.402
50 Rooms, Double: AS 1,900–2,500*
*Includes breakfast & dinner
Open winter & end-May to mid-October
Credit cards: MC, VS
Restaurant closed Mondays
USA Rep: Euro-Connection 800-645-3876
50 km E of Innsbruck

The Hubertushof, a 19th-century hunting lodge, is snuggled on a hillside overlooking the village and lake of Altaussee and beyond to the mountains. Whereas many hunting lodges have an austere façade, this one is as pretty as can be—a lovely, white-stuccoed and wood chalet with cheerful green shutters and colorful geraniums spilling from the balconies. Inside, the walls are adorned with hunting trophies (many collected by the Countess's mother who was an avid hunter). However, the overall ambiance is not that of a masculine hunting lodge but rather of a lovely family home. There is an intimate lounge with a splendid large, antique oil painting of a young mother playing with her children dominating the wall above a cozy grouping of floral slip-covered chairs and sofa. Beyond this parlor is a handsome dining room, richly paneled in pine. There is also an adorable snug bar with a gorgeous dowry chest serving as the counter and a beautiful painted armoire holding the liquor and glasses. Facing the lake is the real heart of the hotel. Here you find an appealing porch with green wicker chairs accented with gay red-and-white-checkered fabric. Upstairs, each meticulously tidy guestroom has its own personality. The gracious Countess Strasoldo spends most of her summers at the chalet, but when she is not in residence her capable manager, Ursula Kals-Friese, continues the same tradition of genuine hospitality, ensuring that everyone feels like a pampered guest.

HOTEL HUBERTUSHOF
Owner: Countess Rose Marie Strasoldo
Puchen 86
8992 Altaussee, Styria, Austria
Tel: (03622) 71.280 Fax: (03622) 71.28.080
14 Rooms, Double: AS 1,100–1,700
Open mid-May to mid-October, Dec 27 to Jan 10,
* February to March, & Easter*
Credit cards: all major
No restaurant: breakfast only
85 km SE of Salzburg

The Seevilla Hotel (an attractive, three-story, cream-colored hotel with intricate green wood trim) has a superb lakefront location—only a pretty lawn dotted with mature shade trees separates it from the Altaussee where the hotel has its own dock. Adding to the idyllic setting, a sparkling mountain stream flows into the lake, embracing one side of the property. The hotel has a whimsical look—sort of a cross between a large Austrian chalet and a Victorian mansion. The Victorian look is a recent phenomenon—a result of lacy green trellis work which was added to the traditional balconies during renovation. At the same time, a large indoor swimming pool was built and, on the floor above it, a spacious dining room with a skylight in the ceiling and large windows on three sides to capture the view of the lake. The swimming pool also has windows opening to the garden and lake. Throughout the public areas there is a refreshing, uncluttered, airy ambiance enhanced by crisp white walls, stripped-wood floors, and light-pine furniture. There are a few antiques for accent, but basically there is a contemporary look. Another nice feature is a large terrace that wraps around two sides of the hotel. When the hotel was remodeled in the early 1990s, new guestrooms were also built. Splurge and ask for one of these prettily decorated rooms in this new wing (such as 108 with a large balcony overlooking the lake). The original guestrooms are also very nice, just not as bright and cheerful.

SEEVILLA HOTEL
Owners: Family Gulewicz
Fischerndorf 60
8992 Altaussee, Styria, Austria
Tel: (03622) 71.302 Fax: (03622) 71.30.28
53 Rooms, Double: AS 1,820–2,690
Open January to October
Credit cards: AX
Restaurant open daily
85 km SE of Salzburg

Badgastein is dotted with huge hotels, built to take advantage of the radium water that makes this mountain town such a famous spa. To reach the Hotel Grüner Baum, continue through town, following signs for the hotel: the road crosses the roaring river, hugs the side of the mountain, and then leaves Badgastein, winding through the mountains to a gorgeous little valley. Here, surrounded by mighty peaks, you find the Hotel Grüner Baum, which has been in the same family for several generations—it was built by Frau Blumschein's entrepreneurial grandmother who had previously run a post hotel in Badgastein. At the turn of the century, when trains replaced horses and buggies to carry the mail, she saw there was no future in a postal stop so, anticipating the growing popularity of spa vacations, she opened a small hotel in the mountains and piped Badgastein's curative water to it. The hotel has expanded over the years and today offers 80 guestrooms. Within the village-like complex there are various lounges, exercise rooms, game rooms, outstanding spa facilities, children's play rooms, and dining rooms (including a special dining room for guests accompanied by their dogs). The attractive bedrooms, located in different chalet-style buildings on the property, are individually decorated. Some, such as suite 118, a beautiful room decorated in blues and yellows, have spectacular views of the mountains. The Hotel Grüner Baum is a deluxe hotel, large yet intimate, offering the charm and hospitality of a family resort.

HOTEL GRÜNER BAUM
Owners: Family Linsinger-Blumschein
5640 Badgastein, Salzburgerland, Austria
Tel: (06434) 25.160 Fax: (06434) 25.16.25
80 Rooms, Double: AS 2,225–3,580
Open mid-December to mid-October
Credit cards: all major
Restaurant open daily
USA Rep: Relais & Chateaux 212-856-0115
104 km S of Salzburg

The Villa Solitude is owned by the Blumschein family who for several generations have operated the Grüner Baum, a sensational hotel located just outside of Badgastein. However, except for the same outstanding quality, the two properties are quite different—each has its own special appeal. Whereas the Grüner Baum is a large resort in a mountain meadow, the Villa Solitude is a small, deluxe hotel in the center of town with the ambiance of a private home. Dating back to the early 1800s, this mansion was for many years the private residence of the Countess of Lehndorff. It was purchased in 1990 by the Blumscheins who proceeded to renovate the house with great love and impeccable taste. The enticing villa is painted a pretty mustard-yellow with white trim and dark-green shutters. In summer, yellow and white flowers framing the house mimic the color scheme. The back of the house looks over Badgastein's famous waterfalls. In summer, meals are served outside on the terrace, looking down to the rushing river. Fine antiques are used throughout—even the bedrooms are brimming with antique furniture. All of the bedrooms are large—many are suites. My favorite is the handsomely decorated Emperor Franz Josef room with its own tiny view balcony. The Villa Solitude is open only in winter, but plans are under way to extend the season. If you are interested in summer accommodations, please check to see if the hotel is open.

VILLA SOLITUDE
Owners: Family Blumschein
Kaiser Franz Joseph Strasse 16
5640 Badgastein, Salzburgerland, Austria
Tel: (06434) 51.010 Fax: (06434) 51.013
6 Rooms, Double: AS 2,200–4,000
Open winter (check with hotel for summer dates)
Credit cards: all major
Restaurant closed Sundays
100 km S of Salzburg

If the thought of slipping back through the ages and living in an authentic romantic castle appeals to you, then we highly recommend the Burg Bernstein. It has everything one dreams of in the castle department—enormous rooms, priceless antiques, a hilltop setting, towers, turrets, an old well, a prehistoric museum, and even a resident ghost. The ghost is the wandering spirit of a beautiful young woman, the wife of a medieval owner of the castle. Her husband became grouchy when he discovered she was in love with her music teacher, so for her indiscretion he promptly walled her up in her room to die. But she is a friendly ghost and you will never be bothered in the comfort of your bedroom— and what rooms they are! A few are just large bedrooms, but most of the accommodations are suites. One of my favorites, Lori, has a handsome antique bed of fine inlaid woods, casement windows overlooking the valley, and a very large, modern bathroom. The castle has passed down through the same family for several generations. Staying here is truly like being a guest in a family home—there are not even keys to the bedrooms. Frau Berger is in charge of the kitchen and her meals, featuring traditional recipes she learned as a girl from the family cook, are exceptional. Breakfast is often served in the central courtyard, while dinner is usually in a magnificent dining room with frescoed walls, deeply recessed windows, and ornate plasterwork. Plan to come and stay awhile—Burg Bernstein makes an excellent base for exploring the castles of Burgenland.

BURG BERNSTEIN
Owners: Family Berger
7434 Bernstein, Burgenland, Austria
Tel: (03354) 63.82 Fax: (03354) 65.20
10 Rooms, Double: AS 1,350–2,000
Four-course dinner AS 290 per person
Open May to mid-October
Credit cards: all major
Restaurant open daily for residents only
100 km S of Vienna

Berwang is a small village of chalet-style houses dotting a lovely high mountain meadow. Like most of its neighbors, the Sporthotel Singer is not an old building, being constructed in 1928 by the Singer family who still own and manage the property. Over the years the hotel has expanded from a simple place to stay to one of sophisticated elegance. If you want to be in the mountains, but do not want to "rough it," then this hotel might be just your cup of tea. Although the overall ambiance has an Alpine flavor, there is nothing remotely rustic in the amenities. From the spacious reception area, an ornate staircase of intricately designed wrought iron and brass sweeps up to a galleried second level where there is a lounge and bar. A huge ornate chandelier drops dramatically down in the open space between the floors. Throughout there is abundant wood paneling, open fireplaces, accents of antique furniture, brocade-covered chairs and sofas, pretty paintings, and beamed ceilings. As you might expect, all of the bedrooms maintain high standards of quality. Half of the accommodations are suites which are extremely popular with guests who come to spend a long holiday in the mountains. In summer, many families come and there is even a playroom equipped with toys for the children. But the very finest aspect of this deluxe hotel is its location—trails through the meadows laced with wildflowers beckon in every direction.

SPORTHOTEL SINGER
Owners: Gerti & Günter Singer
6622 Berwang, Tyrol, Austria
Tel: (05674) 81.81 Fax: (05674) 81.81.83
27 rooms & 27 suites, Double: AS 1,380–3,400
Open May 11 to Oct 6 & Dec 18 to Apr 10
Credit cards: AX, VS
Restaurant open daily
USA Rep: Relais & Chateaux 212-856-0115
75 km NW of Innsbruck, 150 km SW of Munich

What do you do when you suddenly find yourself the owners of a magnificent 12th-century castle? It certainly sounds romantic, but in reality, a castle is an expensive luxury. Such a delightful dilemma faced Christopher Kump when he inherited his grandfather's castle in Austria. Sentimentally reluctant to give up a property where he spent so many happy holidays as a child, yet realistic about the costs involved for upkeep, he and his wife Margaret decided to open the castle as bed and breakfast. It was a natural choice since they are professionals in the hospitality business—owning Café Beaujolais, a famous restaurant in Mendocino, a coastal hamlet in northern California. Although in the near future Schloss Matzen will be open longer, at present it is open only about three months a year, so plan your holiday accordingly because this stunning castle is a "must." The location is excellent—convenient as a hub for day trips to Salzburg, Innsbruck, Kitzbühel, and even Munich. However, once you see the property, you might just want to stay put—the castle is surrounded by 2,500 acres of parkland and has a superb setting on a wooded knoll, looking in every direction to hilltops dotted with castles and, beyond, to the incomparable Alps. The ambiance is truly romantic—nothing trendy or contrived, just authentic antiques throughout, taking you back to days of yore.

SCHLOSS MATZEN
Owners: Margaret Fox & Christopher Kump
6230 Reith, Brixlegg, Tyrol, Austria
Tel: (05337) 62.679 Fax: (05337) 66.581
11 Rooms, Double: $155–225 (US dollars)
Open June, October & February, 2-night minimum
Credit cards: MC, VS
No restaurant, breakfast only, children 13 & older
Reservations made through: Christopher Kump:
 10701 Gurley Lane, Mendocino, CA 95460, USA
 Tel & fax: 707-937-0618, e-mail: cafebeau@mcn.org
40 km NE of Innsbruck, 65 km NW of Kitzbühel

For reasonably priced accommodations in the fairy-tale village of Dürnstein, the Gasthof "Sänger Blondel" offers pleasant rooms, wonderful food, and a great warmth of welcome from the Schendl family who have owned the home since 1640. The gasthof's name is based on the legend of Richard the Lionheart's faithful servant, Sänger Blondel, who discovered his master was imprisoned in Dürnstein castle by playing Richard's favorite song beneath his window. When the king's voice joined in the refrain, the English knew where he was hidden. The inn is enchanting from the first glance—an immaculately kept, pretty yellow house with white trim and dark-green shutters. Wisteria drapes the exterior, potted plants soften the front, and geraniums cascade from windowboxes. The gracious Schendl family give personal attention to each guest and are happy to offer help in planning tours of the surrounding countryside. Several of the staff have been at the inn more than 15 years and know the special requests of returning guests who have become like family, while the same minstrel has been playing his zither in the gasthof for 20 years. There are several attractive dining rooms plus a romantic enclosed garden where you can dine outside, shaded by a giant chestnut tree, and look up at Dürnstein's whimsical church steeple which resembles a blue Meissen porcelain ornament. The pleasant guestrooms vary in size as in a private home, and the price is based accordingly.

GASTHOF "SÄNGER BLONDEL"
Owners: Family Johann Schendl
3601 Dürnstein, Lower Austria, Austria
Tel: (02711) 253 Fax: (02711) 25.37
16 Rooms, Double: AS 940–1,220
Open March to November
Credit cards: none accepted
Restaurant closed 4 pm Sundays & Mondays
84 km NW of Vienna, 6 km W of Krems

Schloss Dürnstein is a magical hotel in a fairy-tale village. This incredibly lovely castle, built by princes in 1630, is blessed with a dazzling location. It nestles high on cliffs overlooking one of the most beautiful scenes in Austria—the Danube weaving its way toward Vienna through the vineyards of the Wachau. Stretching along the side of the hotel that faces the river is a garden terrace where tables are set under the trees for dining. On this romantic perch high above the Danube you could sit forever, enjoying outstanding food, sampling the hotel's own delicious wines, and watching the river traffic. Tucked into another garden, enclosed by stone walls laced with roses, is a swimming pool. In addition, there is a beautiful large indoor pool with murals depicting scenes of the sea. Frau Thiery is in charge of the interior design and the decor throughout is outstanding, abounding with handsome antiques and carefully chosen fine fabrics. The lounges and individually decorated guestrooms all have a formal, gracious elegance. Although Schloss Dürnstein is a deluxe hotel, it is not pretentious in any way. The Thiery family personally manages the hotel and the well trained staff reflect their warmth of hospitality. The Schloss Dürnstein truly sets the benchmark for excellence.

SCHLOSS DÜRNSTEIN
Owners: Rosemarie & Johann Thiery
3601 Dürnstein, Lower Austria, Austria
Tel: (02711) 212 Fax: (02711) 351
38 Rooms, Double: AS 2,500–3,000 *
*Includes breakfast & dinner
Open March 25 to November 8
Credit cards: all major
Restaurant open daily
USA Rep: Relais & Chateaux 212-856-0115
84 km NW of Vienna, 6 km W of Krems

The Pension Halali is just a short walk from the center of Ehrwald, a lovely village located in one of Austria's most beautiful high-mountain valleys. It is easy to spot the pension because in front is a kiosk topped by a small, onion-shaped dome that was brought here from a chapel in the mountains. The white, two-story, chalet-style house with balconies draped with cascading geraniums is not old, but built in the typical character of the region. In front is a sunny terrace where tables and chairs are set for dining. The most outstanding room in this small pension is the stüble which is the epitome of rustic coziness. Here, in an enticing room with log walls darkened with age, you find small tables covered by red-checked tablecloths. Typical carved, wooden Alpine-style chairs and red-checked curtains complete the picture-perfect look. The rest of the house does not have as much rustic personality as the stüble, but everything is spotlessly clean and there are accents of antiques to add to the country flavor. There are also a solarium and a Finnish sauna, which would feel good after a long day hiking in the mountains. The owner, Gerti Sender (who is originally from Munich) bought the pension in 1994 and since then has continued to upgrade the property. For a reasonably priced place to stay in the breathtakingly beautiful valley of Ehrwald, this is a winner.

PENSION HALALI
Owner: Gerti Sender
6632 Ehrwald, Tyrol, Austria
Tel: (05673) 21.01 Fax: (05673) 36.42
30 Rooms, Double: AS 700–870
Open winter & mid-May to end-October
Credit cards: none accepted
Restaurant open daily
70 km NW of Innsbruck, 20 km SW of Garmisch

The Hotel Spielmann has every ingredient to make it one of our favorites: location, charm, amenities, food, history, and, above all—genuine warmth of welcome. Located in a picturesque village in a high mountain valley, the hotel is surrounded by meadows and pastures and has an unobstructed view of the mountains. This is a paradise for children with a swimming pool, playground, and plenty of farm animals about—including two splendid golden-hued Haflinger horses. Inside, the hotel has an unsophisticated, cozy ambiance with hunting trophies, grandfather clock, wooden sled, antique chests, and painted armoires. Each of the bedrooms is individually decorated. Splurge and request one of the rooms in the newest wing (such as 206): these have a bedroom and separate sitting area and are prettily decorated with floral fabrics. The dining room is the heart of the hotel, and the food here is so outstanding that the kitchen has received many awards. Most of the produce, including the meat, comes directly from the farm. The final ingredient of perfection is the wonderful Spielmann family who share their love and knowledge of this beautiful mountain region with their guests. Grandfather Spielmann, who built the original house, was a well-known athlete and the first ski instructor in Austria. His family continues the tradition. Christian is a well-known mountain climber and his two sisters are world-champion powder skiers.

HOTEL SPIELMANN
Owner: Christian Spielmann
Wettersteinstrasse 24
6632 Ehrwald, Tyrol, Austria
Tel: (05673) 22.250 Fax: (05673) 22.255
38 Rooms, Double: AS 1,560–2,480*
*Includes breakfast & dinner
Open winter & end-May to mid-October
Credit cards: all major
Restaurant open daily
70 km NW of Innsbruck, 20 km SW of Garmisch

In every book there are a few favorites—inns that incorporate all the ingredients for a perfect little hotel. The Hotel Alpenrose is such an inn. One of the reasons this hotel is so special is the charm of the owner, Frau Gutwinski, who orchestrates her establishment with grace and skill. She radiates charm and speaks excellent English. In addition to her friendly management, the hotel has many other attributes: it is conveniently located (on a small side street just a block from the heart of the beautiful medieval town of Feldkirch), it is very old (dating back to 1550), and it has many antiques (most inherited from Frau Gutwinski's grandmother who originally owned the hotel). The guestrooms are quite charming—each different and furnished with loving care and with a few well chosen antiques. Those on the top floor (the latest part of the hotel to be renovated) are the most deluxe. Number 31, a suite with windows looking out over the rooftops to the castle on the mountain, is especially romantic. The ambiance throughout is more that of a private home than a commercial hotel. In front of the hotel there is a small square off which you enter into an intimate lobby with a small breakfast room to the left. Breakfast—the only meal offered—is served splendidly on fine china. Lunch and dinner are no problem since there are many excellent restaurants nearby, including a very famous restaurant, the Bären, only a few blocks away.

HOTEL ALPENROSE
Owner: Rosa Gutwinski
Rosengasse 4–6
6800 Feldkirch, Vorarlberg, Austria
Tel: (05522) 72.175 Fax: (05522) 72.17.55
27 Rooms, Double: AS 1,150–1,800
Open all year
Credit cards: all major
No restaurant: breakfast only
USA Rep: Best Western 800-528-1234
160 km W of Innsbruck, 10 km E of Swiss border

Walk back in time through the arched stone doorway leading to the interior courtyard of the Gasthof Deim Zum Goldenen Hirschen. Dating from 1442 and filled with antiques and artifacts, this is an atmospheric inn which overflows with character and history. Wolfgang Deim is the hospitable owner who oversees all aspects of the Gasthof Deim, as his family has done for three generations. We found him supervising the friendly, bustling restaurant where many local families were enjoying a late breakfast. Delicious meals and large steins of thirst-quenching beer are served here on wooden tables amidst stone pillars which support the low, arched, beamed ceiling. A particularly pretty antique ceramic stove warms the restaurant on cold days. Guests are also served in a newly constructed "winter garden" dining room with sliding glass doors which close when it rains. Bedrooms are reached by walking through the flower-filled interior courtyard and hallways decorated with antiques and old prints. Good taste prevails in the bedrooms which are pleasantly furnished in a contemporary country style. Herr Deim's artistic flair and love of history are evident throughout, from strategically placed jugs of flowers to an old apple-wine press and sauerkraut cutter displayed in a stone corridor. The Gasthof Deim Zum Goldenen Hirschen and the colorful walled town of Freistadt make an excellent stop if you are traveling from Austria to the new Czech Republic.

GASTHOF DEIM ZUM GOLDENEN HIRSCHEN
Owner: Wolfgang Deim
Böhmergasse 8
4240 Freistadt, Upper Austria, Austria
Tel: (07942) 72.25.80 Fax: (07942) 72.25.840
32 Rooms, Double: AS 900
Closed 2 weeks end of January
Credit cards: none accepted
Restaurant
40 km N of Linz, just off main plaza

little village of Fuschl lies snuggled in a pocket-sized meadow at the east end schlsee. Because we especially like the Fuschlsee—a small lake close to the busy tourist center of Salzburg, yet with the tranquillity of the countryside—we purposely set out to find a reasonably priced hotel to recommend. How happy we were to discover the Hotel Schützenhof—it really fills the bill. This old hotel is ideally situated in the heart of the village of Fuschl, facing directly onto the lake. Since the building was beginning to show its age, the Vogl family decided to do not just a cosmetic face-lift, but a major renovation. The hotel reopened in April, 1994, and it is as fresh and pretty as spring. The hip-roofed structure is painted a cheerful yellow with white trim, accented on every balcony by windowboxes overflowing with colorful red geraniums. The newly reconstructed portion of the hotel has an appealing contemporary look, with blond-pine furniture, white walls, marble floors, and lovely fabrics on the sofas and draperies. Upstairs, a winter-garden has been added for the use of guests on chilly days. This glass-enclosed room has the feel of a garden, with plants and wicker chairs where guests can enjoy the sun indoors. The hotel has an outdoor terrace for à-la-carte dining just across a pedestrian promenade, and its own private beach only 150 meters away.

HOTEL SCHÜTZENHOF
Owners: Petra & Franz Vogl
5330 Fuschl am See
Salzburgerland, Austria
Tel: (06226) 20.80 Fax: (06226) 56.544
37 Rooms, Double: AS 1,260–1,500
Open all year
Credit cards: none accepted
Restaurant open daily
28 km E of Salzburg

Austria has an unbelievable wealth of villages with incredible settings. One of these is Gargellen, tucked at the end of a narrow valley that dead-ends in soaring mountains (on the other side of these massive peaks is the beautiful Swiss town of Klosters). It is not hard to spot the Alpenhotel Heimspitze—as you drive into town you will see it on your left, just across the rushing glacial stream. The core of the hotel is a century-old farmhouse, but it has greatly expanded over the years as guestrooms and modern facilities have been added. However, the cozy stüble (with walls and low ceiling paneled in wood mellowed with the patina of age) still looks as it did in days gone by. A ceramic stove in one corner, tiny floral prints, pewterware, copper pots, and colorful plates create a charming, rustic ambiance, making guests want to linger with a glass of wine. The paneled dining room is new, but maintains the same rustic character, and the food is exceptional. The guestrooms are simple in decor, but spotlessly clean and attractive. Ask for one of the rooms on the top floor (such as 23) with a balcony looking out to the mountains—the view is beautiful. The Alpenhotel Heimspitze has been in the Thöny family for four generations, and their gracious warmth of welcome and caring are what make this hotel so very special. The Thönys have turned the management over to their son, but Frau Thöny is always about, personally greeting the guests, arranging freshly picked bouquets of flowers, and making sure everyone is pampered.

ALPENHOTEL HEIMSPITZE
Owners: Family Thöny
6787 Gargellen, Vorarlberg, Austria
Tel: (05557) 63.19 Fax: (05557) 63.19.20
15 Rooms, Double: AS 1,540–2,400*
*Includes breakfast & dinner
Open winter & July to October
Credit cards: none accepted
Restaurant closed Mondays to Tuesdays at 3 pm
50 km W of Feldkirch, 168 km SW of Innsbruck

There are so few accommodations to recommend in the northeastern corner of Austria, that we were pleased to find the Alter Schüttkasten. It's not brimming with charm nor decorator-perfect, but, without much competition, it is definitely a winner. The hotel, in fact, has many attributes. The white, three-story building, dating back to the 17th century, was in days of yore the granary for the nearby monastery. It defines its heritage in a building with a steeply pitched roof accented with gabled windows—a well-designed simplicity that is one of the hotel's nicest features. Inside there is a spacious lobby with a small lounge at the end. To the left of the reception is a sky-lit sunroom whose ultramodern decor is a bit jarring. However, the deviation from simplicity stops there. The hotel's very popular restaurant is most attractive, with a handsome vaulted ceiling supported by massive columns, thick walls, antique-style light fixtures, and traditional wooden chairs. The bedrooms too are more than adequate—they are spacious rooms with white walls, built-in headboards and side tables, simple drapes on wrought-iron rods, beamed ceilings, and windows set in walls more than a meter thick. The Alter Schüttkasten does not have the personal touch of an owner-operated hotel, but is well managed and definitely a clean, pleasant stopover.

ALTER SCHÜTTKASTEN
Manager: Josef Steiner
Vorstadt 11
2093 Geras
Lower Austria, Austria
Tel: (02912) 33.20 Fax: (02912) 33.332
26 Rooms: Double: AS 900
Open all year
Credit cards: none accepted
Restaurant open daily
73 km NW of Vienna

The Hotel Seehof (whose origins date back to the 15th century) has been in the Schellhorn family for six generations. Loving care shows in every detail, such as heirlooms artistically arranged in glass display cases, one with great-grandmother's dirndl complete with hat and scarf, another with great-grandfather's Sunday outfit complete with leather britches, fancy hat, and marvelous old pipe. The oldest room in the house is a fabulous, paneled dining room, now used only for special occasions. A modern wing houses the lounge and dining room. The Schellhorns' son, Sepp, is the master chef and has already won many awards for his culinary skills. Guests on the half-pension plan (breakfast and dinner included in the price) are treated to a four- or five-course dinner that includes many menu choices. Should your holiday be in late June, you might be able to sample succulent, fresh wild strawberries, freshly picked in the forest. Behind the hotel, under the shade of two giant chestnut trees, tables and chairs invitingly dot the lawn that stretches down to a small lake where guests may swim. The bedrooms are all extremely pleasant, with stark white walls accentuated by watercolor prints, some by the Swedish artist Carl Larsson. Most of the bedrooms have modern furniture. If you prefer antiques, ask for 29, a room with handpainted chests and beds. If you want a view, ask for 33 or a similar room with a balcony offering an idyllic view of the tiny lake backdropped by mountains.

HOTEL SEEHOF
Owners: Family Schellhorn
5622 Goldegg am See, Salzburgerland, Austria
Tel: (06415) 81.370 Fax: (06415) 82.76
27 Rooms, Double: AS 1,694–1,854*
*Includes breakfast & dinner
Open winter & May to October 25
Credit cards: MC, VS
Restaurant open daily
65 km S of Salzburg

The Schlossberg Hotel is ideally located near the river, just a block from the pedestrian heart of Graz. The tasteful decor of this splendid small hotel is most refreshing. After the ornate, fussy antique furniture encountered in many hotels throughout Austria, the Schlossberg Hotel is like a breath of fresh air. The mood is set by the exterior which is two simple shuttered buildings, one French-blue and one pink. Inside there is a small courtyard, a tiny bar, a comfortable lounge, and two very cozy breakfast rooms. The owner, Herr Marko, is a retired racing-car driver. His attractive wife owns an antique store, and it is her fine taste for simple, predominantly country-style antiques that creates the delightful ambiance. The walls are painted white, contrasting pleasantly with the antique wooden furniture, baskets of fresh flowers, and colorful old oil paintings. The bedrooms offer modern conveniences such as mini-bar, satellite TV, radio, and phone, yet still maintain the country feel, often with antique accents such as beautiful armoires. About 80 per cent of the rooms lead to one of several romantic inner courts. From the terrace on the hillside behind the hotel, reached by taking the elevator to the top floor, the view over the tiled rooftops across the river to the cathedral is spectacular. On one terrace level there is a small swimming pool. The hotel dining room serves only breakfast, but close by there are many restaurants.

SCHLOSSBERG HOTEL
Manager: Simone Schmid
Kaiser-Franz-Josef-Kai 30
8010 Graz, Styria, Austria
Tel: (0316) 80.700 Fax: (0316) 80.70.160
43 Rooms, Double: AS 2,100–3,100
Open all year
Credit cards: all major
No restaurant: breakfast only
Small pool in terraced garden
In the heart of Graz, 202 km SW of Vienna

Rarely have we found a more delightful budget inn than the Deutsches Haus am Almsee. Although tiny (only five bedrooms) and simple (none of the bedrooms has a private bathroom) the hotel is truly charming. Its appeal begins outside—a brown wood chalet-style building accented by green shutters, with a steeply pitched roof, a balcony encircling the second floor, flowerboxes brimming with red geraniums, and a small outdoor patio where meals are served in the summer. From the Deutsches Haus you look across the meadow to the shimmering green Almsee, backdropped by dramatic granite cliffs. Inside, the appealing restaurant has a heavy beamed ceiling, cheerful red draperies, an antique ceramic-tiled stove, and country-style wooden chairs with heart-shaped carvings. Upstairs the bedrooms have washbasins with hot and cold water, but share a bathroom "down the hall." The guestrooms are immaculately clean and cozy with down comforters plumped on the beds. As an added bonus, all of the bedrooms have a view of the lake. Gretel Leithner (the sister of Herr Leithner who runs the nearby Romantik Hotel Almtalhof—see next listing) owns the Deutsches Haus am Almsee and it is her style and excellent taste which make this small inn so special.

DEUTSCHES HAUS AM ALMSEE
Owner: Gretel Leithner
4645 Grünau am Almsee
Upper Austria, Austria
Tel: (07616) 83.32 Fax: none
5 Rooms, Double: AS 660*
*Includes breakfast & dinner
Open winter & May to mid-October
Credit cards: none accepted
Restaurant
125 km E of Salzburg

The Romantik Hotel Almtalhof is a real charmer—especially appealing for guests who love a country ambiance without sacrificing any of the modern amenities. Herr Leithner oversees the efficient operation of the hotel, but he told me it is his attractive wife who is responsible for the appealing decor. Hardly an inch of wall space is left unadorned—dolls, hats, miniatures, statues, wreaths, copper, and etchings artistically decorate the walls. Old sleds, painted cradles, baskets of flowers, wedding chests, and antique armoires accent the rooms. To add a final "homey" touch, Frau Leithner fills all the rooms with her lovely cross-stitching on door plaques, pillows, tablecloths, rugs, and pictures. Not to be outdone, Herr Leithner hand-crafts most of the furniture—what a talented pair! The bedrooms, all pretty, are larger in the newer wing. Room 4 is especially attractive with a beautiful large pine canopied bed, lovely paneled walls, and a small sitting room overlooking the garden. Meals are served either in the cozy wood-paneled dining room or else on the terrace by the river. Either place, the food is delicious—all the produce is fresh from the garden and breads warm from the oven. Since our original visit many years ago, an indoor pool has been added. The Almtalhof is highly recommended: the genuine hospitality of the owners combined with a cozy ambiance, excellent food, and quality throughout make this a real winner.

ROMANTIK HOTEL ALMTALHOF
Owners: Family Leithner
4645 Grünau im Almtal, Upper Austria, Austria
Tel: (07616) 82.04 Fax: (07616) 82.04.66
23 Rooms, Double: AS 2,200
Open winter & May to mid-October
Credit cards: all major
Restaurant open daily
USA Rep: Euro-Connection 800-645-3876
111 km E of Salzburg, 18 km W of Gmunden

Hallstatt is one of the most beautiful towns in Austria—an ancient village clinging to hills that rise abruptly from the waters of the Hallstätter See. In the center of the village is a charming square enclosed by colorful houses and tucked into one of the corners of the square, with its flower-laden balconies just peeking into view, is the Gasthof Zauner. You enter a tiny hallway and then go up a flight of stairs to two very attractive, wood-paneled dining rooms where the food is extraordinary. Grilled specialties always highlight the menu, including, of course, fresh fish. Ask if reinanke (a fish from the Hallstätter See) is on the menu—it is delicious. The Gasthof Zauner has been in the same family for many generations. Zepp Zauner, the manager and chef, is usually the one to greet you and his brother, Warner, a folk singer, frequently helps out. Their delightful father is also sometimes around—if so, ask him about his incredible experiences in World War II. From the dining level, a staircase leads up to the snug, but appealing guestrooms, all furnished in a rustic, regional style with beds, tables, chests, and armoires made from a honey-toned pine native to this area. All have balconies. Room 28 is a very special room with a view out over the rooftops to the lake. Many guests come just for one night, but this is not enough—plan to stay at least several days. Hallstatt makes an excellent base for exploring the many wonders of this region, including the ice caves and prehistoric salt mines that date back to 1200 B.C.

GASTHOF ZAUNER
Owners: Family Zauner
Marktplatz, 4830 Hallstatt
Upper Austria, Austria
Tel: (06134) 82.46 Fax: (06134) 82.468
*12 Rooms, Double: AS, 1,550**
**Includes breakfast & dinner*
Closed November, Credit cards: all major
Restaurant open daily
80 km SE of Salzburg

The resort of Heiligenblut, located just south of the summit of the world-famous Grossglockner Pass, is popular with tourists both winter and summer. Just north of this beautiful little town, set in a hillside meadow, is the Haus Senger, a chalet-style hotel whose dark-wood façade has three tiers of balconies overflowing in summer with brilliant geraniums. As you walk up the hill from the parking lot, you see children playing on the swings on the front lawn while their parents sit on the terrace enjoying the sun and the stunning mountain view. A feeling of warmth and welcome permeates the air. The handsome Senger family are famous for their gracious hospitality and their excellent meals. Be sure to sample the apple strudel—*mit schlagg* (whipped cream), of course. Inside, the hotel is simple with a rustic mountain decor. Especially charming is a small paneled dining room exuding a cozy, old-world ambiance. Following a fire, one wing of the hotel was completely rebuilt and the guestrooms in this new section are especially attractive with a country-Alpine motif. Many of them are suites, very practical for families. The hotel is not old, but built in the traditional mountain-chalet style. What is very special here is the fabulous view and the kindness and hospitality of the owners. Note: Haus Senger is outside the town of Heiligenblut, on the left side of the road as you drive north toward the Grossglockner summit.

HAUS SENGER
Manager: Andreas Senger
9844 Heiligenblut, Carinthia, Austria
Tel: (04824) 22.15 Fax: (04824) 22.159
5 Rooms, 6 Suites, Double: AS 900–1,740
Open end-June to October & Christmas
Credit cards: AX, MC
Restaurant open daily
South of Grossglockner summit, N of Heiligenblut
180 km S of Salzburg, 30 km N of Lienz

Hirschegg is officially an Austrian village, yet you must make a loop into Germany to reach this mountain paradise. The journey is well worthwhile: not only will you pass through some of the most spectacular scenery in Europe, but also discover a jewel of a small hotel. This weathered, wooden farmhouse, dating back to the 16th century, is what you hope to find in the mountains, but so rarely do—an intimate, family-run hotel, filled with antiques and oozing with rustic charm. The mood is set as you enter into the cozy reception area with its low ceiling and massive wooden walls darkened by the patina of age. There are 19 guestrooms, all but one with a balcony capturing a view of the mountains. Each of the bedrooms, although individual in size and decor, has the same country charm with canopy beds and cheerful red-and-white-checked fabric used throughout. Walking sticks, umbrellas, sewing kits, and even bathrobes show the thoughtful attention to detail of the gracious owners. The two dining rooms maintain the same ambiance, with walls and ceilings of age-mellowed paneling and wooden tables and chairs. In warm weather, however, guests usually eat outside on the terrace. For those who want to swim, on the basement level there is a small, grotto-like indoor pool tucked into the rocks with glass doors opening onto the terrace. The Sonnenberg is not the kind of hotel to pop into for one night, but rather a mountain hideaway where you can take long walks each day and become friendly with your fellow guests.

SONNENBERG
Owners: Martine & Kurt Krieger
Am Berg 26, Kleinwalsertal
6992 Hirschegg, Vorarlberg, Austria
Tel: (05517) 54.33 Fax: (05517) 54.33.33
19 Rooms, Double: AS 1,400–1,800
Open winter & mid-May to mid-October
Credit cards: none accepted
Restaurant open daily
75 km W of Bregenz, on hillside above village

If money does not matter, don't even consider the Jagdhof am Fuschlsee—stay at the super deluxe Schloss Fuschl located on the lake just a bit farther down the road (both hotels are owned by the same company). Although the Schloss Fuschl is an incomparable property, the Jagdhof is an excellent compromise for those on a budget. The hotel is a large stuccoed-and-timbered, two-story building, brightly accented in summer by red geraniums. It resembles the wealthy farmhouses which dot the landscape, and, indeed, it was a farm in years gone by. After a major fire, the hotel was completely rebuilt on lines true to its heritage. Although it faces directly onto the main road 158, the hotel backs onto a pretty golf course and, beyond, the Fuschlsee. The interior of the hotel has the motif of a hunting lodge with an abundance of trophies and antlers. There are also accents of antique furnishings, but the overall feel is one of a fresh, pretty, beautifully decorated commercial hotel. There is a country-style dining room to the left as you enter, plus a more formal, paneled restaurant in the back, looking out to the distant lake. In summer, when the weather is warm, the favorite place to dine is on the spacious deck that wraps around the building. The nicely decorated bedrooms have a traditional hotel look. Some guestrooms are in the Jagdhof, others just down the road in the equally attractive annex which also houses several conference rooms and an indoor swimming pool.

JAGDHOF AM FUSCHLSEE
Manager: Milli Linzmayr
5322 Hof bei Salzburg, Salzburgerland, Austria
Tel: (06229) 23.720 Fax: (06229) 23.72.413
57 Rooms, Double: AS 1,500–1,800
Open all year
Credit cards: all major
Restaurant open daily
USA Rep: Best Western 800-528-1234
25 km E of Salzburg, 4 km E of Hof

The location of the Schloss Fuschl is idyllic—the beautiful 15th-century castle nestles on a wooded peninsula that stretches into the Fuschlsee. The public rooms are located in the main castle—the beautiful lounge (with vaulted ceiling, massive fireplace, antique furnishings, and exquisite tapestries) is especially outstanding. The dining rooms are also lovely and have windows overlooking the lake. Schloss Fuschl has a total of 84 bedrooms, including 7 spectacular, antique-filled suites which are located in the original castle. If you want to splurge, you will truly feel like royalty in suite 6, an opulently decorated, spacious corner room overlooking the lake. But if your pocketbook does not stretch to a suite, do not worry—all the individually decorated bedrooms (located in adjacent buildings and lakefront bungalows) are extremely appealing. Schloss Fuschl has a well-equipped spa, a "beauty farm," tennis, and golf. In addition, a path leads through the trees down to a wooden pier that stretches along the lakefront—a favorite spot for guests to sun and swim. One of the nicest features of this super deluxe hotel is that, in spite of the elegance of the property, there is no hint of pretentious grandeur—none of the haughty air sometimes experienced at world-class properties. The staff are well trained and exceptionally friendly.

SCHLOSS FUSCHL
Manager: Stefan Lauda
5322 Hof bei Salzburg
Fuschlsee, Salzburgerland, Austria
Tel: (06229) 22.530 Fax: (06229) 22.53.531
84 Rooms, Double: AS 3,700–6,600
Open all year
Credit cards: all major
Restaurant open daily
USA Rep: LHW 800-223-6800
26 km E of Salzburg, 5 km E of Hof

Perched high in an unspoiled Alpine meadow above the town of Imst, the Alpenhotel Linserhof enjoys an idyllic setting. The small lake nestled in the meadow in front of the hotel invites peaceful contemplation or a quiet walk. Cared for with pride by the Linser family, the Alpenhotel Linserhof is a large structure of dark wood and white plaster built in chalet style. Charm is added by the numerous balconies overflowing with red geraniums. The restaurant is obviously a very popular dining spot, and its enclosed porch dining area affords lovely, peaceful views of the surrounding Alps. A varied menu offers traditional Austrian dishes as well as Italian specialties. A large flagstone terrace overlooking the Alpine panorama is a wonderful place to relax with an afternoon beer, a large Austrian flag flying overhead. On a cold or cloudy day, enjoy lunch or dinner in the warm, wood-paneled dining room, decorated with paintings and drawings by a local artist interspersed with numerous hunting trophies. Dramatic wrought-iron accents and dark, beamed ceilings complete the typical Austrian ambiance. The bedrooms are divided into two sections: one building is mostly family apartments, while the other has mostly double rooms, all of which are beautifully furnished, many with balconies. Room 107 is an especially lovely corner room decorated in tones of pinks and greens. Further guest amenities include an indoor, heated swimming pool, sauna, library, and a billiard room. Swimming in the little lake is also very enjoyable. The Alpenhotel Linserhof is a splendid choice for its warmth of hospitality, tranquil setting, and glorious views.

ALPENHOTEL LINSERHOF
Owners: Family Linser
6460 Imst, Tyrol, Austria
Tel: (05412) 66.415 Fax: (05412) 66.41.51.33
35 Rooms, Double: AS 1,360
Open all year
Credit cards: all major
Restaurant open daily
40 km W of Innsbruck, 2 km N of Imst

The Romantik Hotel Post began its history over 500 years ago as the "Schloss Sprengenstein," then later it became an important post station. For over 100 years it has been a hotel owned for four generations by the Pfeiter family (on my last visit, I spotted the fifth generation, little Christina, peacefully sleeping in her bassinet behind the reception counter). From the moment you walk up a flight of stairs to the main lobby, the mood is of quality and refinement: tasteful antiques abound. Most of the furniture is of the formal, somewhat stiff Biedermeier period except for one cozy little dining room which is decorated in country style with rustic wooden furniture and paneled walls. The formality also disappears completely as you enter onto a romantic, trellised veranda, laced with ivy and accented by boxes of brightly colored flowers, which wraps around the side of the hotel. Here meals are served looking over the expansive gardens and the swimming pool and beyond to the mountains. Whether served on the veranda or in the main dining room, the food is delicious. The bedrooms are pleasantly furnished—not in antiques, but in a tasteful, traditional style. This old inn has had many additions over the centuries, the latest being a new wing and an indoor swimming pool.

ROMANTIK HOTEL POST
Owners: Family Pfeiter-Raggl
6460 Imst, Tyrol, Austria
Tel: (05412) 66.554 Fax: (05412) 66.51.955
30 Rooms, Double: AS 950–1800
Open February to November
Credit cards: all major
Restaurant open daily
USA Rep: Euro-Connection 800-645-3876
40 km W of Innsbruck

The Goldener Adler is ideally located in the pedestrian heart of Innsbruck. Its prime position is no coincidence—the inn was built near the ancient bridge that spanned the River Inn. This crossing was on the main route connecting northern and southern Europe and the Goldener Adler was built to house the many guests traveling this road. Strategically positioned Innsbruck was one of the main stops along the way and it seems that every historical personal of any importance stayed here at one time. The guest list is most impressive: Emperor Maximilian I, Charles V, Kaiser Joseph II, Mozart, and Goethe were among just a few who spent the night here. Even today, a tone of times-long-past permeates the hotel. Although completely renovated in 1990 (to celebrate the hotel's 600th birthday), nothing was done to destroy the historical ambiance. On the ground level is a series of cozy dining rooms, looking much as they must have done hundreds of years ago. One floor up is a large, more formal dining room, a real beauty with beamed ceiling, pretty blue drapes on wrought-iron rods, and blue tablecloths. The bedrooms vary in size and shape as this is an old building, but the dark-wood furniture made by artisans in Innsbruck is similar in all. One exception is 208, the "Bridal Suite"—if you feel like splurging, ask for this especially attractive, large corner room. It is bright and cheerful, with wooden floors accented by throw rugs, light-pine four-poster bed draped in white fabric, matching desk and tables, and carved, Alpine-style chairs.

GOLDENER ADLER HOTEL
Manager: Friedrich Mang
Herzog-Friedrich Strasse 6
6020 Innsbruck, Tyrol, Austria
Tel: (0512) 58.63.34 Fax: (0512) 58.44.09
35 Rooms, Double: AS 1,600–2,100
Open all year
Credit cards: all major
Restaurant open daily
Heart of old town, near Alte Innbrücke (bridge)

The Romantik Hotel Schwarzer Adler is located just a few minutes' walk from the pedestrian heart of medieval Innsbruck. The inn's history dates back to 1500 and public records verify that it has had a checkered past, performing such functions as a coaching inn, a nobleman's palace, a royal skittle alley, a pub, and even a stable housing 60 coaches and 120 horses. Since the beginning of the 20th century, the Schwarzer Adler has been a proper inn, continuously run by the Ultsch family. Today Sonja and Harald Ultsch (fourth generation) have taken over management of the hotel—and since they have three children, the family tradition of hospitality is sure to go on. The mood is not that of a formal, deluxe hotel, but rather one of great friendliness with a homelike, old-fashioned ambiance throughout. The reception area, located one floor up from ground level, is intimate and the staff dedicated to giving personal service. Each of the guestrooms is individual in decor. The ones I liked best were those with a rustic Alpine flair. If you want a quiet room, request one facing the rear—such as 337, which overlooks a garden terrace and has pretty-light pine furniture. The most romantic room in the Schwarzer Adler is its outstanding restaurant, which oozes old-world charm. Here a beamed ceiling, handsome dark-wood wainscoting, stained-glass windows, antique clocks, and a collection of copperware set the mood for elegant dining by candlelight.

ROMANTIK HOTEL SCHWARZER ADLER
Owners: Sonja & Harald Ultsch
Kaiserjägerstrasse 2
6020 Innsbruck, Tyrol, Austria
Tel: (0512) 58.71.09 Fax: (0512) 56.16.97
26 Rooms, Double: AS 1,500–2,300
Open all year
Credit cards: all major
Restaurant open daily
USA Rep: Euro-Connection 800-645-3876
Heart of Innsbruck, just outside city walls

The 16th-century Weisses Rössl is not a deluxe category hotel, but is definitely a marvelous choice for a place to stay in Innsbruck. Its location in the pedestrian section of the old part of the city is superb. The hotel is an attractive, dove-gray building with white trim, windowboxes of red geraniums, and a jaunty, wrought-iron sign embellished with a white horse jutting out above the arched stone doorway. The hotel is not on ground level, but one floor up where you find the reception area and public rooms. Here there are two dining rooms with windows overlooking the street. My favorite is the stüble with beamed ceiling, hanging lamps, and rustic wooden chairs with cushions made from a cheerful pink-and-green-floral fabric which is repeated at the windows. Adjoining is a second dining room, also very attractive, with the same rustic ambiance: wooden furniture, paneled walls, and hunting trophies on the walls. In warm weather, guests dine outside on a pretty little terrace accented by yellow umbrellas. The simple bedrooms are all similar in ambiance—fresh-looking and uncluttered, with blond-colored, wooden built-in beds and side tables, bentwood chairs, framed prints on white walls, and good reading lights. Best of all, everything is spotlessly clean and well kept. This delightful small hotel has been in the gracious Plank family for three generations, a tradition which will be continued by the son and daughter who now also help with the hotel.

WEISSES RÖSSL
Owners: Rosemarie & Werner Plank
Kiebachgasse 8
6020 Innsbruck, Tyrol, Austria
Tel: (0512) 58.30.57 Fax: (0512) 58.30.575
13 Rooms, Double: AS 1,200–1,400
Closed 2 weeks April & November
Credit cards: all major
Restaurant closed Sundays & holidays
Heart of old town, near Alte Innbrücke (bridge)

Winter or summer, the Hotel-Pension Zur Linde is a small, homey hotel where one can relax and be enveloped by Herr and Frau Patscheider's genuine hospitality. Their picturesque, gable-roofed, balconied house is located on a sunny corner in the small ski town of Hungerburg, 6 kilometers north of Innsbruck. In the early spring, the front terrace and garden are filled with skiers sunning themselves, as the Zur Linde enjoys an ideal location across the street from the gondola which operates year round to accommodate hikers and sightseers. The house is filled with family treasures—lovely old oil paintings by local artists and hanging wood sculptures depicting the ancient legends of this mountainous region. If asked, Frau Patscheider is happy to relate these fascinating stories to guests in her excellent English and Herr Patscheider will proudly show his magnificent collection of rare old prints and documents relating to Austria's historic hero, Andreas Hofer. The four guest bedrooms and two suites are simple, containing antique or pine furniture and homey touches such as paintings on the walls and a good-night chocolate on the pillow. All rooms have balconies and sink areas, but when making your reservation, remember that only half have a private bathroom. However, if you are on a budget, the rooms without a private bathroom are a good value.

HOTEL PENSION ZUR LINDE
Owners: Family Patscheider
6020 Innsbruck-Hungerburg, Tyrol, Austria
Tel & fax: (0512) 29.23.45
6 Rooms, Double: AS 760–1,400
Open all year
Credit cards: all major
No restaurant: breakfast & snacks only
Funicular from Innsbruck
6 km N of Innsbruck

The Gasthof Zur Traube is a traditional country inn dating from 1313. Incredibly enough, the house has been in the Raitmayr family for 16 generations, and today is still a beloved family concern, managed by Hans Raitmayr, his pretty wife, and his two brothers. The charm of this inn is not immediately apparent in the wide entry hall, but once through the wooden doors leading to any of the three cozy dining rooms, visitors are rewarded by the sight of low, beamed or carved wooden ceilings and warm pine-paneled walls, all with a rich patina which comes only with time. Each of the dining rooms is slightly different: one has an old ceramic stove, another a collection of old pewter plates and mugs. Pretty tablecloths and fresh flowers dress the tables, and a wide variety of wines and carefully prepared dishes are offered. Upstairs, the wide hallways are a bit bare, but lead to comfortable bedrooms, all with private bath. Many of the fresh, well-kept guestrooms are furnished in contemporary knotty pine. If you prefer antiques, ask for one of the rooms furnished with painted furniture that has been handed down in the Raitmayr family for many generations. Most rooms have flower-bedecked balconies looking out to spectacular views of the surrounding Tyrolean scenery. A friendly gathering spot for locals and a haven for the Raitmayrs' faithful returning clientele, the Gasthof Zur Traube is a historic, yet highly comfortable inn from which to explore the Innsbruck area.

GASTHOF ZUR TRAUBE
Owners: Family Raitmayr
6072 Lans 9, Tyrol, Austria
Tel: (0512) 37.72.61 Fax: (0512) 37.72.61.29
26 Rooms, Double: AS 920
Closed October 10 to November 4
Credit cards: all major
Restaurant open daily
6 km S of Innsbruck

The setting of the Hotel Grunwalderhof is breathtaking—high on a plateau overlooking a beautiful green valley whose soft meadows are accentuated by a backdrop of gigantic rocky mountains. The favorite rendezvous for guests is the grassy terrace behind the hotel where chairs dot the green lawn—a perfect spot for soaking up the sun and the stunning view. From this terrace, a path leads off to a swimming pool in the garden which is an oasis on warm summer days. The view must have been the motivation of the Counts of Thurn when they chose this site on a high mountain plateau to build their hunting lodge. The Hotel Grunwalderhof still embraces its past: this is not a fancy deluxe hotel, rather a comfortable "homey" lodge reflecting its hunting heritage. There are antiques accenting all of the rooms, but the basic decor is a sporty motif with antlers and hunting mementos decorating the walls. The bedrooms vary considerably in size and decor: most are quite simple. It is the setting that makes this hotel so very special.

HOTEL GRUNWALDERHOF
Owner: Gerda Seiler
6082 Patsch, Tyrol, Austria
Tel & fax: (0512) 37.73.04
27 Rooms, Double: AS 990–1,620
Open May to mid-October
Credit cards: all major
Restaurant closed Mondays
6 km S of Innsbruck

Even among Austria's superb selection of castle hotels, the Schloss Kapfenstein stands out as very special. Like most fortified castles, it crowns the crest of a hill. Just before reaching the top, you pass a lovely small yellow church, then around one final bend of the road, and you are at the outer gates of the castle. You will undoubtedly be welcomed by a member of the extremely gracious Winkler family. Eva Winkler previously did all the cooking, but now her son Martin (a most talented young chef) has taken over in the kitchen while his wife, Elizabeth, helps serve. Meals are usually enjoyed outside on a terrace that stretches along the top of the castle walls: a setting that offers a stunning panorama of rolling hills, vineyards, forests, and quiet villages. In the distance you can see both Slovenia and Hungary. Another son, Georg, (ably assisted by his wife, Margot) oversees the vineyards. His excellent wines are both served and sold at the hotel. If you have an interest in the grapes of this region, Georg will give you a tour of his cellar and advise you of other wineries in the area to visit. The guestrooms are all appealingly furnished in a comfortable, homey way. If you want to splurge, ask for the suite—it has a bedroom with antique furniture, separate sitting room, and a gorgeous view. The Schloss Kapfenstein makes no pretense to be a fancy hotel, but it is truly a gem. For genuine hospitality, wonderful food, fine wines, incredible views, and a tranquil setting, this is really tops. Stay at least several days to explore this beautiful niche of Austria.

SCHLOSS KAPFENSTEIN
Owners: Family Winkler-Hermaden
8353 Kapfenstein, Styria, Austria
Tel: (03157) 22.02 Fax: (03157) 22.024
9 Rooms, Double: AS 1,760–1,800*
*Includes breakfast & dinner
Open April to December
Credit cards: none accepted
Restaurant open daily
67 km SE of Graz

The Hotel Strasshofer is located on the main street of the picturesque little town of Kitzbühel, a colorful walled Tyrolean village dating back 700 years. The entrance to the Hotel Strasshofer does not hold much promise—just a nondescript, street-front hallway facing the main pedestrian street of Kitzbühel. It is not until you walk up a flight of stairs that you have any inkling of how nice this small hotel really is. On the second level, you find a lobby and two very attractive, cozy dining rooms: one has a hunting motif with antlers decorating white walls above wooden paneling, the other has light wooden chairs and pretty gay curtains. Another flight of stairs leads to the bedrooms. All of the guestrooms are pleasing in decor, but some are especially appealing, decorated in what is called *bauer mobel* style (with farmer-style furniture). These rooms cost a little more, but are really lovely, with rustic-style canopied beds, light-pine tables and chests, and colorful provincial-print fabric used for the draperies and the slipcovered chairs and sofas. There is a sauna in the hotel for the use of guests. The greatest asset of this inn is the price—very reasonable for Kitzbühel.

HOTEL STRASSHOFER
Owner: Franz Strasshofer
6370 Kitzbühel
Tyrol, Austria
Tel: (05356) 22.85 Fax: (05356) 71.532
20 Rooms, Double: AS 1,500–1,700
Open January to October
Credit cards: all major
Restaurant open daily
Heart of Kitzbühel
120 km E of Innsbruck, 80 km SW of Salzburg

Romantik Hotel Tennerhof is an idyllic hotel snuggled in the foothills of the mountains, just outside Kitzbühel, one of Austria's most picturesque walled villages. The location is terrific—close enough to walk into town, yet far enough removed to feel as though you are in the country. If you come in summer, the appealing chalet-style exterior is as pretty as a picture postcard with balconies draped with geraniums. Inside, the perfection continues, with lovely antiques abounding in every nook and cranny. The decor throughout is one of sophisticated country charm. Every detail is faultless: every fabric and piece of furniture is thoughtfully chosen and perfectly placed both in the public areas and the bedrooms. The von Pasquali family, who own the hotel, also meticulously oversee every phase of its management—and it shows. There are three lovely dining rooms, and, as might be expected, the food is delicious. The hotel has expanded over the years as new enhancements and bedrooms have been added. The latest wing houses some spacious new guestrooms, spa facilities, and a lovely indoor pool. There is also an outdoor pool terraced in the garden below the hotel. The Romantik Hotel Tennerhof is definitely a hotel where you will want to linger—relax by the pool, take leisurely walks along lovely meadow paths, hike into the mountains, and explore the colorful walled village of Kitzbühel. If you are on a winter holiday, the skiing is superb.

ROMANTIK HOTEL TENNERHOF
Owners: Family von Pasquali
Griesenauweg 26
6370 Kitzbühel, Tyrol, Austria
Tel: (05356) 31.81 Fax: (05356) 31.81.70
42 Rooms, Double: AS 1,900–3,600
Open winter & June to October
Credit cards: MC, VS
Restaurant closed Wednesdays
USA Rep: Euro-Connection 800-645-3876
120 km E of Innsbruck, 80 km SW of Salzburg

The Hotel zur Tenne, ideally located in the heart of charming Kitzbühel, reopened in December 1995 after a total renovation. The metamorphosis is astounding—the hotel has been transformed from a simple place to stay to a world-class star that will appeal to the most discriminating guests. The hotel is made up of three separate houses, each cheerfully painted—one in rust, one in blue, and one in mustard-yellow. Tables and chairs set on a street-side terrace offer a choice spot to enjoy afternoon tea and watch the parade of people passing by. For cooler days, there is also a glass-enclosed "winter garden" restaurant stretching across the front of the hotel. The tone of the hotel is set from the moment you enter. The reception area exudes a rustic charm tempered by a sophisticated elegance. The floor is brick, inset with blue ceramic tiles, while the ceiling and walls are handsomely paneled in light pine, as is the beautifully carved reception counter. Although this is a deluxe hotel, the efficiently trained staff are extremely friendly. To the right of the reception area is a cozy bar and, beyond, a superbly decorated dining room. The sophisticated "country look" prevails with a large fireplace along one wall and chairs upholstered in an appealing blue plaid fabric. Throughout the hotel, there are many lovely Tyrolean antiques such as painted armoires and dowry chests. The bedrooms are also outstanding, with a cozy, rustic appeal. On the lower level of the hotel there is a well equipped health spa.

HOTEL ZUR TENNE
Manager: Egon F. Michelitsch
Vorderstadt 8-10
6370 Kitzbühel, Tyrol, Austria
Tel: (05356) 44.44 Fax: (05356) 48.03.56
51 Rooms, Double: from AS 1,650
Open all year
Credit cards: all major
Restaurant open daily
Heart of Kitzbühel, 100 km SE of Innsbruck

Frequently I have introduced a hotel as being a famous restaurant offering a few bedrooms, but the Romantik Hotel Musil is even more unique: its claim to fame is as a fabulous bakery–offering a few bedrooms. Dominating the corner of the hotel is a beautiful bakery with marvelous pastries that can be purchased either to take home or to eat in the adjacent café. The reception desk faces both the lobby and the bakery: when the shop is busy, the attendant scurries back and forth to service both sides. Passing through the lobby, you come into a circular glass-domed atrium, a bright, sunlit room where meals are served. There is also a café and a more formal dining room with a hunting motif. The bedrooms are large, clean, and comfortable with a combination of simple decors: some have copies of painted furniture, others have a few antiques. The Romantik Hotel Musil is a good choice if you are looking for a small hotel in the heart of the old city of Klagenfurt, and an especially appealing choice if you like pastries.

ROMANTIK HOTEL MUSIL
Owner: Bernd Musil
10 Oktober-Strasse 14
9020 Klagenfurt
Carinthia, Austria
Tel: (0463) 51.16.60 Fax: (0463) 51.67.65
12 Rooms, Double: AS 2,400–3,000
Open all year except Christmas
Credit cards: all major
Restaurant open daily
USA Rep: Euro-Connection 800-645-3876
Located at the heart of Klagenfurt

For a reasonably-priced place to stay in Lech, the Pension Alpenland is truly a jewel. It is newly built in the Tyrolean style—a pretty white chalet with wood trim, carved balconies, green-shuttered windows, and flowerboxes spilling over with red geraniums. The location is perfect—just a few minutes' walk from Lech's main street, yet looking out to the mountains over meadows of wildflowers. Although the exterior is attractive, it is what you find within that sets the Pension Alpenland apart from the many similar chalets nearby. The gracious owner, Priska Jochum, has both a talent for decorating and a flair for making guests comfortable. From the moment you enter you find a romantic mood enhanced by Oriental carpets, beautiful chests, hats hanging on the walls, fresh flowers, painted armoires, spinning wheels, and antique dolls. But there is no clutter: everything is fresh and pretty. Beyond the reception area is the attractive dining room, retaining the country motif with paneled walls and ceiling. In summer only breakfast is served, although in winter dinner is also available. The bedrooms are located on the three upper floors, those on the top level tucked cozily up under the eaves. The comfort and ambiance rival many of the deluxe hotels in town. Frau Jochum has added her personal touch and each room is individually decorated and very pretty. Many of the bedrooms have balconies, but one of my favorites, number 10 (decorated in a floral fabric of pink, green, and yellow) has no balcony but an especially pretty view of the mountains.

PENSION ALPENLAND
Owner: Priska Jochum
6764 Lech, Vorarlberg, Austria
Tel: (05583) 23.51 Fax: (05583) 31.805
17 Rooms, Double: AS 980–1,500*
*Includes breakfast & (except in summer) dinner
Open winter & end-June to October
Credit cards: none accepted
Restaurant open winter; summer breakfast only
100 km W of Innsbruck, 62 km E of Feldkirch

There are no compromises in quality at the Hotel Arlberg: this is truly a deluxe hotel in every sense of the word. You will be pampered from the moment you arrive, with excellent food served in beautiful dining rooms, tasteful antique decor in the public rooms, and attractively furnished bedrooms with excellent modern baths. The nicest feature of the Hotel Arlberg is that in spite of being a very sophisticated operation, it definitely maintains the personality of a family-loved and -operated small hotel. The Schneider family built the hotel and they are definitely involved with its management. In summer a cocktail party is given once a week on the terrace where several generations of the gracious Schneider family mingle with their guests. It seems every year some imaginative new improvements such as indoor and outdoor pools, tennis, and sauna are added to further enhance the property. The location is also superb: the hotel snuggles in a bend of the Arlberg river that weaves through the center of Lech, one of the most picturesque ski resorts in Austria. Lech is most famous for its skiing, but summer is equally lovely with a grand selection of beautiful walking trails through the high mountain meadows.

HOTEL ARLBERG
Owners: Family Schneider
6764 Lech, Vorarlberg, Austria
Tel: (05583) 21.340 Fax: (05583) 21.34.25
46 Rooms, Double: AS 2,500–2,900*
*Includes breakfast & dinner
Open winter & July to mid-September
Credit cards: none accepted
Restaurant for guests open daily
100 km W of Innsbruck, 62 km E of Feldkirch

The Hotel Post has a prime location on the main street as you drive into the charming mountain village of Lech. It is only a short walk from the hotel to the gondola station, convenient in winter for skiing and in summer for a lift to the high mountain meadows for walking. It is not surprising that the location is so superb since this former post station was one of the town's first hotels. It has expanded over the years, adding many modern-day improvements, but the cozy exterior has not changed: it looks the same as in the last century—a gaily painted building with green shutters and lacy stenciling adorning the plaster façade. In summer the hotel is even more enchanting with red geraniums cascading from the windowboxes. Most of the buildings in Lech are of new construction, but the Hotel Post is one of the few remaining old buildings and it happily retains its old-world atmosphere inside with the use of wood paneling, country rustic-style furniture, pewter plates on the walls, hunting trophies, cozy fireplaces, and many pieces of antique furniture. The bedrooms vary in style but many maintain the rustic country feeling with new Alpine-style painted furniture and gay, provincial-print draperies. The gracious Moosbrugger family own and operate this historic hotel.

HOTEL POST
Owners: Family Moosbrugger
6764 Lech, Vorarlberg, Austria
Tel: (05583) 22.060 Fax: (05583) 22.06.23
38 Rooms, Double: AS 2,430–3,500
Open winter & July to mid-September
Credit cards: none accepted
Restaurant open daily
USA Rep: Relais & Chateaux 212-856-0115
100 km W of Innsbruck, 62 km E of Feldkirch

The Hotel Post, an old postal station, tucked into a small square just behind Lermoos's picturesque church, has been in the Dengg family since the 1700s. The hotel also has an annex across the street, the Postschlössl, a handsome square mansion built by the wealthy postmaster and predating the Hotel Post by 200 years. Although the Postschlössl has great character (especially its wide, vaulted central hallway guarded by suits of armor), ask for accommodations in the Hotel Post because here, without a doubt, you will be treated to one of the finest views in all of Austria. You enter into a spacious lobby with walls accented by mirrors and old paintings, wood-beamed ceiling, and Oriental carpets on tiled floors. There is a jewel of little stüble, paneled completely in antique wood. The newer section of the hotel maintains the same character, with lounges and dining rooms offering a rustic charm with white walls, golden-hued wooden furniture, and many antiques. The guestrooms are divided into two categories, the "Tyrol" rooms and the "Zugspitze" rooms. Ask for one of the "Zugspitze" rooms—these cost a bit more, but are worth it. Each of these simply furnished bedrooms has a balcony that captures a panoramic view across an expansive green meadow backdropped by the soaring mountain peaks. This same stunning vista is also the highlight of a large terrace (built above the indoor swimming pool) behind the hotel. Small tables are set for dining or just a drink while guests soak in the magical splendor of this mountain paradise.

HOTEL POST
Owners: Family Dengg
6631 Lermoos, Tyrol, Austria
Tel: (05673) 22.810 Fax: (05673) 22.81.41
54 Rooms, Double: AS 940–1,060
Open winter & May to November
Credit cards: MC, VS
Restaurant open daily
47 km NW of Innsbruck, 31 km SW of Garmisch

Women especially will relate to the history of the Hotel Traube which begins, "Each generation (since 1586) has built and improved something in order to satisfy the guests with comfortable rooms as well as a good cuisine and drinks. This achievement was basically due to the fact that the Vergeiners (the owners) got their wives and housemothers from good landlord families." Whether this successful operation is indeed due to the fact the Vergeiner men married good strong women or not, the fact remains that today the hotel is splendidly managed. When you first see the hotel you might be disappointed because the side which faces the parking area is quite modern, but inside, the old-world ambiance quickly asserts itself with liberal use of quality antiques. As you walk through the hotel and out the opposite entrance that faces Lienz's quaint pedestrian shopping street, all hesitations are dispelled. This side of the hotel is charming—a rust-colored façade, windows trimmed in crisp white, dark-green shutters, and, in front, a gay blue-and-white-striped awning protecting a delightful outdoor café. The bedrooms are large and comfortably furnished. The hotel remains the best in Lienz for both tourists and business travelers.

ROMANTIK HOTEL TRAUBE
Owner: Günther Wimmer
Hauptplatz 14
9900 Lienz, Tyrol, Austria
Tel: (04852) 64.444 Fax: (04852) 64.184
48 Rooms, Double: AS 2,100–2,500
Open all year
Credit cards: all major
Restaurant open daily
USA Rep: Euro-Connection 800-645-3876
147 km W of Klagenfurt, 180 km SE of Innsbruck

Ritterburg Lockenhaus is a characterful old castle on the top of a small mountain in the province of Burgenland, reached by a road that winds up through a densely forested hill. Just before attaining the pinnacle you go through an ancient doorway to an inner courtyard which on sunny days is a scene of much gaiety, with wine, beer, and good food being served at wooden tables. A door leads off to the right of the courtyard to a tavern-style dining room where excellent cold beer and hearty meals are served in cozy surroundings. The reception desk is in a small room close to the entrance and nearby stairs lead up to six freshly painted bedrooms, some with antique beds and beautiful views. Except for the wonderful old beds, the furnishings are not outstanding, but the views certainly are very special. (Rooms 3 and 4 are especially attractive.) There are also 29 rooms in an annex down the hill so, when making a reservation, be sure to specify you want a room in the castle. The castle is also open to the public as a museum, so you can combine your night's stay with sightseeing. The Ritterburg Lockenhaus is not a family-run hotel, so lacks the personal touch and warmth of welcome that the nearby Burg Bernstein provides, but for an inexpensive place to stay, it is a good choice.

RITTERBURG LOCKENHAUS
Manager: Horvath Eugen
7442 Lockenhaus, Burgenland, Austria
Tel: (02616) 23.94 Fax: (02616) 27.66
6 Rooms, Double: AS 890–1,100
Open February to December 24
Credit cards: none accepted
Restaurant open daily
Open to public as museum
120 km S of Vienna

The exterior of the Hotel Post is picture-postcard-perfect, doing justice to the colorful village of Lofer. The pretty white chalet-style hotel is enhanced by green shutters, painted detail around the windows, wooden balconies, and flowerboxes overflowing with cheerful red geraniums. Inside, the lobby is simple, but leading off to the left is a charming little breakfast room with mellow paneled walls, simple wooden chairs with rounded backs, comfy country-print cushions, and blue curtains at the windows. The bedrooms are furnished with simple wooden furniture, rag rugs on the floors, and fluffy down comforters on the beds. I was told that some of the best guestrooms have antique wooden furniture, so when making a reservation, be sure to request one of these. This is a very simple hotel—certainly not suitable for those seeking luxury—but the town of Lofer is extremely attractive and the Hotel Post is a most picturesque little inn. It is located on the main street, facing a little square, just steps away from many beautiful small shops, many specializing in Tyrolean-style clothing.

HOTEL POST
Manager: Christine Soucek
5090 Lofer
Salzburgerland, Austria
Tel: (06588) 303 Fax: (06588) 308
30 Rooms, Double: AS 550–750
Open May to November
Credit cards: all major
No restaurant: breakfast only
48 km SW of Salzburg

The Landhaus Kellerwand is primarily known for its restaurant, rated as one of the top ten in Austria. Although the owner, Sissy Sonnleitner, is one of the country's finest chefs, this appealing inn has far more to recommend it than just the food. The Landhaus Kellerwand is a large pastel-yellow, two-story house with a small tower on one corner. Except for flowerboxes at the windows, the building reflects the style of an English manor more than the chalet style so prevalent in Austria. The ambiance inside is a happy marriage of cozy comfort and natural elegance. The core of the house is an enclosed garden courtyard, a quiet haven with a small fountain, walls draped with wisteria, green shrubbery, and statues. Looking into this inner garden is a cozy sitting area with a large fireplace and chairs and sofas slip-covered in a red-and-green-floral fabric. The attractive dining room for hotel guests also has windows looking into the garden. There is a second à-la-carte restaurant decorated in soft tones of green and yellow. Throughout the hotel are many fine antiques, but nothing is stiff or formal—a homey comfort prevails. The spacious bedrooms are not as antique in ambiance as the public rooms, but also display the charm of a private home. Landhaus Kellerwand, which goes back at least 500 years and has been passed down through a line of daughters for many generations, is located in the mountain village of Mauthen near the Italian border (on 110, just beyond Kötschach).

LANDHAUS KELLERWAND
Owners: Sissy & Kurt Sonnleitner
9640 Mauthen-Kötschach 24
Carinthia, Austria
Tel: (04715) 269 Fax: (04715) 37.816
12 Rooms, Double: AS 1,700–2,200*
*Includes breakfast & dinner
Open mid-December to mid-November
Credit cards: all major
Restaurant open daily for hotel guests
38 km SE of Lienz, 1 km S of Kötschach

The Hotel Garni Prem is a picturesque Tyrolean house which is fastidiously looked after by the Prem family. Attired in her traditional dirndl, Elisabeth Prem is an attractive and hospitable Austrian hostess who speaks very good English. Her family's pretty, early-18th-century chalet is located in the heart of Mayrhofen on a side street leading off the main square where the village church is found. Bright red rose bushes border the lush green lawn and fruit trees shelter the walkway to the front door. The lower windows are bordered by fresco paintings and the top two floors are ringed by light-wood balconies and vari-colored geraniums. The Prem family is documented as having been in Austria since 1320, and many of their family antiques are displayed in the hotel. These painted chests and armoires, old paintings, prints, and Oriental rugs add character to the public areas. The cozy, wood-paneled dining rooms invite guests to linger over a delicious breakfast before a day of winter skiing or summer hiking. A good night's rest is assured in the 28 comfortable, very clean bedrooms, all with private bath. All rooms also offer a romantic balcony for gazing out over the incomparable mountain scenery. In warm weather the tranquil back garden is a perfect setting for a leisurely game of cards, a good book, or quiet contemplation.

HOTEL GARNI PREM
Owner: Elisabeth Prem-Fankhauser
6290 Mayrhofen, Tyrol, Austria
Tel: (05285) 22.18 Fax: (05285) 37.41
28 Rooms, Double: AS 800
Closed November
Credit cards: none accepted
No restaurant: breakfast only
70 km SE of Innsbruck

The Die Forelle, a resort hotel built at the turn of the century, has 75 rooms, which makes it larger than most of the places featured in this guide. However, because the Aniwanter family care so much, it reflects the same warmth of welcome and personalized service as those inns with only a few guestrooms. The Aniwanters are always present, catering to the needs of their guests. What a difference it makes when the owner is on the premises, overseeing every detail of management from bouquets of fresh flowers to the immaculate maintenance of the rooms. The ambiance throughout has a genteel, understated quality— nothing trendy or the last word in decorating, just good, old-fashioned, traditional comfort and excellent service. Bedrooms are located in two buildings that join to form this lakefront hotel. The Die Forelle has a prime location on a peninsula which curves gently into the Millstätter See. Surrounding the hotel, colorful displays of flowers bloom in well tended gardens, and facing the lake is a swimming pool. Also fronting the lake is a spacious terrace where guests can enjoy an excellent meal in a most romantic setting. The hotel has two tennis courts, and there is boating and swimming in the lake. If you want to take a circle tour of the lake, which you should certainly do, it is a pleasant walk along a promenade that hugs the shoreline to the pier from where ferries frequently depart.

DIE FORELLE HOTEL
Owners: Family Aniwanter
9872 Millstatt, Millstätter See
Carinthia, Austria
Tel: (04766) 20.500 Fax: (04766) 20.50.11
75 Rooms, Double: AS 1,400–1,900
Open May to October
Credit cards: none accepted
Restaurant open daily
45 km NW of Villach

The Hubertus Schlössl has a fabulous lakefront location in the colorful resort of Millstatt. When seen from the lake, the small castle looks like a fantasy with steeply pitched, tiled roof, perky gabled windows, turrets, and even a small tower. Although the style reflects the Victorian period (the hotel dates back to 1894), there is also a definite Austrian flavor. It is painted a bright yellow, has dark-green shutters, and, of course, the ubiquitous display of red geraniums. The mood within is one of a hunting lodge, with many trophies accenting the paneled walls. Both the combination bar-lounge and the dining room have a masculine, Victorian look with heavy, dark-wood furniture, enormous hunting prints, and paneled walls. But the ambiance changes in the cheerful, glassed-in sun terrace with pretty white furniture and windows on three sides overlooking the lake. There is also an outdoor dining terrace looking on to the lake. There are many antiques in the public rooms, but the guestrooms are more modern. If you want to splurge, ask for the room with a small balcony overlooking the lake. The ambiance throughout is definitely that of a private home, which it was until bought by several families from Millstatt. The property is manage by the Hohenwater-Sodek family who own the nearby Seewirt Hotel. When making reservations, you are actually calling the Seewirt Hotel, so be sure to specify you want a room in the Hubertus Schlössl.

HUBERTUS SCHLÖSSL
Managers: Family Hohenwater-Sodek
Kaiser Franz Joseph Strasse 49
9872 Millstatt, Millstätter See, Carinthia, Austria
Tel: (04766) 21.10 Fax: (04766) 21.10.54
18 Rooms, Double: AS 1,820–2400*
*Includes breakfast & dinner
Open June to October
Credit cards: none accepted
Restaurant open daily
45 km NW of Villach, lakefront

Millstatt is a colorful old town built on the slope of a hill rising from the Millstätter See. Our other recommendations in Millstatt are directly on the lake, but the Hotel Post is located in the middle of the old town, on a small street near the main square. Most of the resort hotels that have sprung up around the lake are attractive but recently built with a modern appearance, but the Hotel Post has been a guesthouse for over 100 years. The hotel, a square building whose mustard-yellow façade is accented with white trim and dark-green shutters, conveniently faces the village with its array of small shops. Just a short stroll down the hill and you are at the lakefront where swimming, boating, and ferry excursions are all available. For guests who prefer swimming in a pool, there is a nice one in the garden behind the hotel. The dining room is attractive, with a cozy ambiance of paneled walls and ceiling, wooden tables and chairs, intricately designed wrought-iron chandeliers, and fresh flowers on all the tables. The hotel has been enlarged and although we usually recommend the old section of hotels, at the Hotel Post the newer bedrooms are nicer: most have balconies and an attractive traditional decor. The Hotel Post has another feature rarely found in hotels—the Sichrowsky family has a nanny who supervises a nursery for their children and those of hotel guests.

HOTEL POST
Owners: Family Sichrowsky
9872 Millstatt
Millstätter See, Carinthia, Austria
Tel: (04766) 21.08 Fax: (04766) 27.77
37 Rooms, Double: AS 1,600–2,000*
*Includes breakfast & dinner
Open May to October
Credit cards: none accepted
Restaurant open daily
45 km NW of Villach

When you catch your first glimpse of the Burg Oberranna perched romantically in the wooded hills above the Wachau Valley, it will be love at first sight. Once you are across the moat and through the castle gates, the enchantment only increases. When the Nemetz family originally saw the castle, they too were quite taken with its singular beauty. At that time the elderly owner was not ready to sell, but on that first visit, a certain inexplicable rapport developed between the elderly lady and the Nemetzes' little girl, and years later, when forced by health to sell, the owner remembered the Nemetzes and wanted them to have her home. When they took over, the castle was in sad disrepair and had only one bathroom. Luckily, Herr Nemetz is a talented architect and has sensitively restored the castle into the gem you see today. The decor is outstanding, with antiques used throughout in a way that creates a relaxed, friendly ambiance. Just off the cozy tavern (where in winter a roaring fire warms the room) is a superb terrace stretching to the castle walls. Here tables and chairs are set so that guests can savor the view down the Wachau Valley far below. Of the twelve rooms, seven are suites. Because the rooms are so popular with guests who come for an extended stay, Frau Nemetz is understandably reluctant to book a room far in advance for one night, but you can always call close to the time you want a reservation and if space is available, there is no problem. However, the best solution is just to make this your hub for your explorations of this lovely area

BURG OBERRANNA
Owners: Lydia & Roland Nemetz
3622 Mühldorf, Lower Austria, Austria
Tel: (02713) 82.21 Fax: (02713) 83.66
12 Rooms, Double: AS 1,400–1,700
Open May to November
Credit cards: AX, VS
Restaurant open daily for hotel guests only
Located on Danube 108 km W of Vienna

Gralhof Pension, a delightful small inn, is located across the road from the emerald-green Weissensee. It has its own grassy lawn stretching down to the lake where a wooden pier is available for swimming, boating, or fishing. The hotel is a farmhouse dating back 500 years—one of the oldest farmhouses in the valley. The lower part of the building is of white stucco and the upper portion constructed of wood. Wooden balconies with carved banisters and windowboxes overflowing with red geraniums encircle the inn. The inside is immaculate. Most of the light-pine furniture is new but there are accents such as an antique cradle, antlers, deer skins, wedding chests, red-checked curtains, and family portraits giving a country flavor. The food is country-simple and delicious. Frau Knaller, who is extremely gracious and speaks English very well, was cooking dinner when we arrived. The smells from the kitchen were enticing and she explained that her husband is a farmer and all the milk, butter, cheeses, and vegetables are fresh. Before dinner you might want to take a short walk down the road and board one of the ferries which circle the lake.

GRALHOF PENSION
Owners: Family Knaller
Neusach, 9762 Weissensee
Carinthia, Austria
Tel: (04713) 22.13 Fax: (04713) 22.13.75
18 Rooms, Double: AS 1,200–1,380*
*Includes breakfast & dinner
Open winter & May to mid-October
Credit cards: none accepted
Restaurant open daily for guests
170 km S of Salzburg, 56 km E of Villach

The Alpenrose is located high above the Millstätter See with a glorious panorama of rolling hills, small farms, villages, meadows, and forests, with the highlight being the beautiful Millstätter See in the distance. Although most of the hotel is of new construction, an old-world, cozy ambiance oozes from every nook and cranny. When you investigate further, you find that the heart of the Alpenrose incorporates a 300-year-old farmhouse, complete with darkened, heavy-beamed ceilings, a snug fireplace, and a breakfast nook in a sunlit bay window. The bedrooms continue the romantic mood set by the dining and sitting rooms, with light-pine rustic furniture and provincial-print fabrics. Decorated with the same country charm, a large, attractive room on the top floor is set aside for yoga or exercise classes. For health-conscious guests, there are also splendid, state-of-the-art spa facilities and a swimming pool—and you will certainly want to get some exercise because the food is irresistible: it is delicious and beautifully presented. Butter and cheeses come from the farm, bread is warm from the oven, soups are homemade, vegetables are fresh from the garden, and everything is prepared without the use of preservatives. When the weather is warm, meals are served outside at tables set with pretty linens on a wide terrace with a stunning view. The owners are the crowning glory of this small gem of a hotel—their charm, genuine warmth of welcome, attention to detail, and quality of excellence are unsurpassed.

HOTEL ALPENROSE
Owners: Family Obweger-Theuermann
9872 Obermillstatt, Millstätter See, Carinthia, Austria
Tel: (04766) 25.00 Fax: (04766) 34.25
30 Rooms, Double: AS 2,240–2,800*
*Includes breakfast & dinner
Open all year
Credit cards: none accepted
Non-smoking house
49 km NW of Villach, in hills above Millstatt

From the outside, the Gasthof Zum Stern is one of Austria's prettiest small hotels. This 18th-century, ochre-colored inn is almost entirely embellished with intricate paintings. The picture-postcard look is further enhanced by windows framed with lacy designs and, above the front door, a fabulous projecting six-sided oriel window beneath which flowerboxes dance with red geraniums. When you come inside you might at first be disappointed because the lobby is starkly simple, but one of the three dining rooms offers all the charm promised by the appealing exterior: the wooden walls are mellowed dark with age, a plump ceramic stove nestles in the corner, antique pewter plates line the shelves on the walls, and rustic hand-carved antique chairs surround sturdy wooden tables. The dining room in the new wing of the hotel is much more modern in mood. The food is hearty and very good—prepared from the local fresh produce and fruits. There are 12 bedrooms on the second floor: these are fairly large and immaculately clean, but do not expect too much decor—the furnishings are ultra-simple and the bathrooms are made of one-piece molded plastic. However, these guestrooms are most satisfactory for a budget inn—especially one with such an outstanding façade and pretty dining room.

GASTHOF ZUM STERN
Owner: Josef Griesser
Kirchwege 6
6433 Oetz, Tyrol, Austria
Tel & fax: (05252) 63.23
12 Rooms, Double: AS 790*
*Includes breakfast & dinner
Open all year
Credit cards: none accepted
Restaurant for guests open daily
50 km SW of Innsbruck

The Ossiacher See is well known as a haven for campers whose colorful tents dot every available meadow around the lake. Until the Stiftshotel Ossiach opened its doors in 1993, the few simple hotels around the lake lacked character, but now that has all changed. The Stiftshotel Ossiach is built within the walls of the Ossiach Benedictine Abbey, which was first documented in 689. On the property (but not a part of the hotel) there is an exquisite church, a masterpiece of gilded baroque design. The location of the Stiftshotel is perfect—it is just two minutes' walk along a garden path to the dock where you can climb aboard a ferry to explore the lake. The hotel also has its own private park next to the lake (guests have their own key to the locked gate). Here you find a large lawn with deck chairs, a play yard for children, a swimming pier, and even a little rowboat for the use of guests. The decor in the public rooms is simple, not like that in a deluxe hotel (but then, remember, the price is reasonable). However, the architectural embellishments are delightful: the breakfast room with its fabulous vaulted ceiling has special charm. When the weather is warm, dinner is served outside on the terrace, a most romantic spot with many flowers and a view of the lake. There are only 25 guestrooms, and all are very large. If you book well in advance, you might be lucky enough to snare room 211, an outstanding corner bedroom overlooking the lake. Austria's second-largest music festival is held at the abbey each summer, when rooms might be hard to reserve.

STIFTSHOTEL OSSIACH
Manager: Stephan Hillhouse
9570 Ossiach, Ossiacher See, Carinthia, Austria
Tel: (04243) 86.64 Fax: (04243) 86.648
25 Rooms, Double: AS 1,500
Open May to October
Credit cards: all major
Restaurant open daily
Located 14 km NE of Villach, on lake

The 400-hundred-year-old Hotel Plomberg-Eschlböck is a gourmet restaurant with rooms. What fun to savor a meal featuring fine food and wines, and then be able to push your chair from the table and walk upstairs for a contented night's sleep. Food is the star attraction at the Hotel Plomberg. It is hard to imagine that this tiny inn, tucked across the road from the Mondsee, only a short drive from Salzburg, can offer what is considered by many experts to be the finest food in Austria. The owner, Karl Eschlböck, is also the chef and his culinary creations are not only delicious, but so artistically arranged on the plate that momentarily one hesitates to destroy the beauty of the design. There are four dining rooms, each loaded with charm. There is also a carved bar set in a cozy nook decorated with baskets of fresh flowers and an antique grandfather clock. There are ten nicely decorated guestrooms (plus an apartment). The bedrooms that have a balcony offer a lovely view of the lake and the big linden tree in front of the house, but are not as quiet as those in the back since the road runs below. Plomberg is difficult to find as the town is not marked on most maps but if you take the Mondsee exit from the A1 and follow the 154 along the west side of the lake, you will see a signpost to Plomberg.

HOTEL PLOMBERG-ESCHLBÖCK
Owners: Monika & Karl Eschlböck
Plomberg, 5310 Mondsee
Upper Austria, Austria
Tel: (06232) 31.66 Fax: (06232) 31.66.20
10 Rooms, Double: AS 900–2,200
Open all year
Credit cards: AX, VS
Restaurant closed Mondays & Tuesdays
* December to March*
33 km E of Salzburg, on W shore of the Mondsee

The Schloss Leonstein, a beautiful castle hotel, is located on the busy main street of the small lake resort of Pörtschach. However, once you have entered into the spacious property, you are insulated from the hustle and bustle of the town. The park like grounds are lovely: not only is this old castle surrounded by lawns, but flower gardens are tucked into the small courtyards where large trees, walkways, and ivory-colored walls please the eye. In summer, chamber music concerts are frequently given in one of the courtyards. The reception area is light and airy with beautiful antiques. The dining room is also very attractive, with vaulted ceilings, Oriental carpets, and high-backed upholstered chairs. Most important, the food is rated among the best in Austria. The guestrooms have been recently refurbished and are charming. One of my favorites, the Johannes Brahms room (where Brahms supposedly stayed), is romantically furnished in antiques. Schloss Leonstein is across the street from the lake and has its own private lakeside park where towels, lockers, lounge chairs, and small boats are available for the use of guests, along with a small restaurant. From the hotel it is also an easy walk to the pier where you can board one of the ferries which circle the lake.

SCHLOSS LEONSTEIN
Owner: Christoph Neuschelle
Pörtschach, 9210 Wörther See
Carinthia, Austria
Tel: (04272) 28.160 Fax: (04272) 28.23
30 Rooms, Double: AS 2,380
Open mid-May to October
Credit cards: AX, VS
Restaurant open daily
On Wörther See, 10 km W of Klagenfurt

The Schloss Seefels, built in 1860 as a private estate, makes a wonderful place to break your journey through southern Austria. This super-deluxe hotel is imbued with a tasteful, classic elegance. Some expensive hotels do not seem to justify their room rates: not so with the Schloss Seefels—everything is perfect. Here you can relax and be pampered for a few days in supreme tranquillity while soaking in the beauty of the Wörther See. A grassy lawn slopes from the hotel to the lake where a wooden pier stretches over the water for sunbathing and swimming. Boats are docked for water sports with an attendant to assist with boat excursions, water-skiing, or wind-surfing. An indoor pool stretches from within the hotel out onto the lawn, thus accommodating swimmers on either cool or sunny days. The large bedrooms are beautifully furnished with color-coordinated spreads, drapes, sofas, and chairs. The dining room is especially attractive: a very large airy room with one solid wall of French doors that open out into a lake-view balcony with white wrought-iron tables and chairs set for summer dining. Tennis enthusiasts will love the well-kept courts. Although this is an elegant resort, there is no feeling of aloof grandeur—the staff are kind, friendly, and gracious.

SCHLOSS SEEFELS
Owner: Constantin Dumba
Toschling 1
Pörtschach, 9210 Wörther See
Carinthia, Austria
Tel: (04272) 23.77 Fax: (04272) 37.04
75 Rooms, Double: AS 3,430–4,830
Open winter & mid-April to mid-October
Credit cards: all major
USA Rep: Relais & Chateaux 212-856-0115
On Wörther See, 12 km W of Klagenfurt

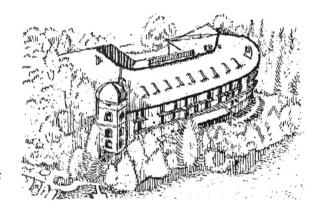

Our guides never feature places to stay with only one guestroom. However, the Zur Gruberstube is so very special that there is no question—we must share it with you. Anyway, there is not *just one* bedroom—there is a suite with two bedrooms, a bathroom, a living room, and even a small kitchen (an ideal situation for a family or friends traveling together). The true focus of the Zur Gruberstube is its restaurant: there are two stunning dining rooms, both brimming with cozy charm. The delightful old farmhouse dates back to 1772 and has been in the same family for countless generations. It had fallen into disrepair when the attractive Christine Prugger came "home" in 1994 and took over the massive job of renovation. With dedicated attention to preserving her heritage, she authentically restored the house and filled it with country antiques. Christine is an artist and her talent is self-evident in her flair for decorating. The beamed-ceilinged dining rooms and reception hall are picture-perfect, with red-checkered cushions, Oriental carpets, bouquets of fresh flowers, spinning wheels, clocks, oil portraits, antique plates, wedding chests, and hand-painted armoires. The setting of this picturesque inn is also sensational. The view from the front is over the valley and beyond to the mountains, while, almost behind the house, the wooded hills rise quickly to rugged mountain peaks. This lovely little inn is one of the best values in Austria. Come and plan to stay awhile.

ZUR GRUBERSTUBE
Owner: Christine Prugger
Gruberhof 51, Vordere Ramsau
8972 Ramsau am Dachstein, Styria, Austria
Tel: (03687) 81.759 Fax: none
1 Suite, AS 600 (2 persons), AS 1,200 (4 persons)*
*Breakfast not included
Open all year (must call ahead in winter)
Credit cards: none accepted
Restaurant closed Thursdays
90 km SE of Salzburg

The Schloss Rosenau is well known as the first headquarters of the Freemasonry Lodge and is open as a museum. In the 18th century the ideals of Freemasonry were an important part of Austria's political, social, and artistic life and Wolfgang Amadeus Mozart composed much Masonic music—*The Magic Flute* reflects Masonic symbolism. From the outside the castle is very pretty: a three-story, pale-yellow building with white trim and a fancy tower in front crowned with a jaunty clock tower. Inside, the castle loses much of its fairy-tale glamor and becomes more commercial. To the right of the entrance hall is the ticket office for tours of the castle and also the reception counter for the hotel. To the left of the entrance hall is a series of rather bland dining rooms to serve not only guests of the hotel, but also the many tourists who come to visit the hotel's museum. A staircase leads up to the first floor which is dedicated to the museum. Again, the interior design of the castle is not as grand as the exterior would imply. There must have been a shortage of money when the decoration was done long ago since many of the walls were painted to imitate beautiful paneling and marble. The floor above the museum has 18 guestrooms, one of which (number 18) has handsome, dark-wood antique furniture. All the others are similar in decor, with blond, light-wood built-in furniture. The accommodations are more than adequate and since there are so few hotels available in this niche of Austria, this is one of the best choices.

HOTEL SCHLOSS ROSENAU
Manager: Helmuth Weber
3924 Rosenau, Lower Austria, Austria
Tel: (02822) 582.21 Fax: (02822) 582.18
18 Rooms, Double: AS 1,240–1,450
Open all year
Credit cards: all major
Restaurant open daily
105 km NW of Vienna, 6 km W of Zwettl

Rust is our favorite village around Burgenland's Neusiedler See. There are several large hotels here built along the lake, but none as charming as the tiny Rusterhof snuggled next to the church and facing directly onto the main square lined with gaily painted houses. The Rusterhof (dating back to 1535) had previously served as a school and is one of the oldest of the many charming old houses in Rust. It was bought by an architect, Matthias Szauer, who renovated the house with great sensitivity, maintaining its original character while adding all the modern conveniences. It is an extremely pretty house with a red-tiled roof accenting the creamy-white façade and with tables and chairs in front. The Rusterhof is mainly a restaurant and is divided into several intimate, cozy dining rooms plus a lovely walled garden terrace where guests dine outside in warm weather. There is also a very old vaulted stone wine cellar that is used for special parties. The guestrooms are all suites, or, more accurately, small apartments since they all have kitchenettes. If you are traveling with friends or children, the two-bedroom apartments would be perfect. If you are just a twosome, request the *Kirchengartenblick* (church garden view) suite, a large bedroom with a sitting area and a kitchenette. Although each of the suites has a different floor plan, they all have the same ambiance—a fresh, pretty, uncluttered look. The furniture and floors are light pine while the walls and fabrics are in tones of white.

RUSTERHOF
Owner: Matthias Szauer
Rathausplatz 18
7071 Rust, Burgenland, Austria
Tel: (02685) 64.16 Fax: (02685) 64.16.11
4 Suites, Double AS 850–1,150
Closed December
Credit cards: none
Restaurant closed Wednesdays
75 km SE of Vienna

Just outside the very popular tourist destination of Saint Wolfgang (immortalized in Benatzky's operetta *The White Horse Inn*), the Landhaus zu Appesbach shares the same lovely lake, but avoids the busloads of tourists who throng the town each day. The attractive, pastel-yellow, two-story building, laced with ivy and accented by green shutters, seems more English than Austrian in appearance. This is not surprising since the original owner (who built the Appesbach at the turn of the century as his home) was an Anglophile. The hotel, surrounded by woodlands and lush lawn, is perched on a slight hill that slopes gently down to the waterfront where there is a pier for boating and a swimming dock. The interior is not decorator-perfect, but very comfortable. The Appesbach is not a stiff, formal hotel, but rather one where the guest is made to feel truly at home. Meals are served in an attractive dining room stretching across the front of the hotel with windows overlooking the lake. Even better, there is a view terrace where guests can dine outside when the weather is warm. The hotel offers a wide spectrum of accommodations, all the way from luxurious to family apartments. If you want to splurge, number 20 is an especially pretty room with floral-patterned drapes and a balcony overlooking the lake. If you are on a tight budget, the Appesbach also offers some super-value, very small, romantic rooms tucked under the eaves. A personal favorite is room 9 with a window giving a side view through the trees out to the lake.

LANDHAUS ZU APPESBACH
Hosts: Brigitte von Kozma & Maximilian Eidlhuber
5360 Saint Wolfgang, Salzkammergut, Austria
Tel: (06138) 22.09 Fax: (06138) 22.09.14
26 Rooms, Double: AS 1,250–2,500
Open March to January
Credit cards: all major
Restaurant open daily
USA Rep: Euro-Connection 800-645-3876
50 km E of Salzburg, 1 km E of St. Wolfgang

In 1992 a new gem was added to the hotel scene in Salzburg, the Hotel Altstadt Radisson SAS. Do not be put off by the fact that it is part of a hotel chain—this is in no way your lackluster commercial hotel. The Altstadt is built within three historical houses that face the River Salzach. The building, first mentioned in 1377, was a brewery from the 15th century until the 1900s. After extensive renovation, the hotel is now a superbly run, deluxe hotel imbued with an old-world ambiance. From the moment you enter, an understated, refined elegance surrounds you. Instead of a large, impersonal lobby, the space is broken into intimate sitting areas which provide quiet nooks to relax. One floor up is the dining room stretching across the length of the building with windows looking out to the river. At the far end of the dining room is a glassed-in winter garden where round tables surrounded by comfortable blue wicker chairs set a cozy atmosphere. There are 60 charming guestrooms, each individually decorated with the finest-quality furnishings. One of my favorites (405) is an especially spectacular corner room with a tiny, wrought-iron "Juliet" balcony for enjoying the river view. Convenient for sightseeing, the hotel faces into the heart of the old part of Salzburg—no need for a car: you can walk everywhere. Note: Drive to the riverside entrance and park in front of the hotel. The porter will take your car to the garage.

HOTEL ALTSTADT RADISSON SAS
Manager: Heidi Peters
Rudolfskai 28/Judengasse 15
5020 Salzburg, Austria
Tel: (0662) 84.85.710 Fax: (0662) 84.85.716 or 718
60 Rooms, Double: AS 2,600–6,400
Open all year
Credit cards: all major
Restaurant open daily
USA Rep: Radisson Hotels 800-333-3333
Middle of Old City, facing river

If you are looking for a small hotel in the heart of Salzburg that offers true charm and warmth of welcome, yet does not cost a fortune, the Elefant is a fabulous choice. This gem of a small hotel is tucked into a narrow side street off the Getreidegasse, Salzburg's famous, colorful shopping street. The hotel is named for an elephant brought over the Brenner Pass in 1552 as a gift to the Emperor Maximilian II. Of course, almost no one in Austria had ever seen an elephant and he caused such a stir of excitement that several inns along the route were renamed "Elefant" to commemorate the event. The house is over 700 years old and has been documented as an inn for the past 400 years. The hotel has been in the Mayr family for several generations and it is their tradition of extending to guests true Austrian hospitality that makes this inn so special. Frau Mayr is personally involved with the management, seeing that guests are made welcome. Herr Mayr is the chef (there are three restaurants associated with the hotel, so he is very busy). The lobby of the hotel is extremely appealing, with a small reception counter, a cozy grouping of chairs and sofa, a splendid antique desk, and a harlequin-patterned marble floor accented by an Oriental carpet. In addition to this sitting area, there is a beautiful private lounge for guests upstairs which exudes a welcoming, home-like ambiance. Because the building is so old, the bedrooms naturally differ in size and shape, but all are attractively decorated in a traditional style.

HOTEL ELEFANT
Owners: Family Mayr
Signumd-Haffenergasse 4
5020 Salzburg, Austria
Tel: (0662) 84.33.97 Fax: (0662) 84.01.09.28
36 Rooms, Double: AS 1,290–1,820
Open all year
Credit cards: all major
Restaurant open daily
Middle of Old City, ½ block off Getreidegasse

From the moment you see the welcoming sign with the gold deer hanging over the front door and enter into the cozy reception hall of the Hotel Goldener Hirsch, you will be enchanted. Everyone from the doorman in his green apron to the maid in her crisp uniform greets you warmly and wishes you a pleasant day. Just beyond the front desk there is a central patio with a glass ceiling where the friendly bartender is ready to fix you a refreshing drink. For more substantial fare, there is a traditional restaurant in the hotel plus, just a few steps down the street, a less formal restaurant, the Herzl, also owned by the hotel. This second restaurant has a cozy ambiance, with dark, rustic wood walls and heavy-beamed ceilings. It seems the hotel grew like an adolescent—in spurts. Rooms are tucked away in all kinds of little nooks and corners. It might take a while to remember just how to get to your room as it could involve a couple of elevators and a jumble of corridors, but once you have arrived you will be delighted. Although some bedrooms are quite small, they are all charming. Most of the rooms are decorated in tones of dark green and rose and combine a few antiques with more recently designed hand-crafted furniture.

HOTEL GOLDENER HIRSCH
Manager: Count Johannes Walderdorff
Getreidegasse 37
5020 Salzburg, Austria
Tel: (0662) 80.84 Fax: (0662) 84.33.49
71 Rooms, Double: AS 3,680–7,680
Open all year
Credit cards: all major
USA Rep: Relais & Chateaux 212-856-0115
Middle of Old Salzburg

The Pension Herbert is a charming, well kept pension located on a busy main street about a 15-minute walk or short bus ride from the center of Salzburg. Herr Herbert Lindpointner is the solicitous host who speaks excellent English. He also owns the cozy café next door which serves delicious cakes and coffees as well as savory lunches and dinners. The pension is an attractive yellow-with-white-trim building which has always been a guesthouse since it was built in 1880. A wide wooden staircase leads upstairs to the twelve tastefully furnished bedrooms, ten of which have clean and modern private baths. Painted antique chests and armoires decorate the hallways, while the bedrooms feature Bavarian-style reproduction furniture. Careful attention to detail is evident in the good lighting, complementing curtains, carpets, and wallpapers, and atmospheric paintings that brighten all the bedrooms. Breakfast is served in the traditional dining room on the first floor which has heart-carved wooden chairs and fresh flower posies on each table. The original pine benches built around its perimeter add to the warmth of the room. Herr Lindpointner and his Pension Herbert offer comfortable accommodation at a reasonable price, perfect for the traveler seeking a more homey atmosphere in city accommodation.

PENSION HERBERT
Owner: Herbert Lindpointner
Nonntalerhauptstrasse 87
5020 Salzburg, Austria
Tel: (0662) 82.03.08 Fax: (0662) 82.03.085
12 Rooms, Double: AS 980–1,300
Closed February
Credit cards: all major
No restaurant: breakfast only
1 km from Mozartplatz

The Hotel Kasererbräu is a good choice for a reasonably priced hotel with a convenient central location in the heart of Old Salzburg (only a few minutes' walk from Mozartplatz). You climb a few stairs from the street level to the lobby where a reception desk is located at the end of the room. Off the reception area is a garden terrace. There are also a prettily decorated breakfast room and a somewhat somber lounge with antique furniture where guests congregate to exchange sightseeing tips and tell of their day's adventures. The hotel is well known to Americans, so you should find many English-speaking guests. The Hotel Kasererbräu is very old, so naturally the bedrooms vary greatly in size and decor, but they are pleasantly decorated and some have antique furniture. Especially attractive is number 24, a room with Tyrolean-style painted furniture. Other rooms feature fancy Biedermeier furniture—if you prefer one of these antique-style bedrooms, indicate your preference when making your reservation and be aware that they are only available in the superior category. During high season (July, August, and September) maximum rates apply and there is a three-night minimum stay.

HOTEL KASERERBRÄU
Owners: Family Giebisch
Kaigasse 33
5020 Salzburg, Austria
Tel: (0662) 84.24.45 Fax: (0662) 84.24.45.51
43 Rooms, Double: AS 1,650–2,600
Open all year
Credit cards: all major
Restaurant closed Sundays
Middle of Old Salzburg

The Hotel Österreichischer Hof, dating back to 1866, is located just across the river from the historical heart of Salzburg (easily accessible by a pedestrian bridge). From the exterior, the large, peach-colored building does not hint at its interior charm, but when you walk inside, you see that the hotel has great character. The reception area is a spacious, rather formal room with a handsome mosaic tiled floor. Looking up you see a giant skylight and a series of galleried floors off which are the guestrooms. Beyond the lobby is a very warm and gracious bar and sitting room—quite elegant, with chairs and sofas upholstered in beautiful fabric in tones of deep pink, creams, and green that sets off to perfection the dark-wood paneling. Beyond the bar is a sun room with windows looking out to the river. In addition to a rather formal restaurant, there is a charming dining room that looks as if it is straight out of a hunting lodge. The lower part of the walls and also the ceiling in this cozy room are paneled in a handsome wood. Hunting trophies, oil paintings, and carved chairs give the final touch of rustic charm. The bedrooms are all outstandingly decorated with traditional furniture and lovely fabrics, and have large marble bathrooms. The ambiance in all the guestrooms exudes refinement and great taste. If you want to splurge, choose one of the deluxe doubles (such as 301) which are exceptionally large and have balconies overlooking the river.

HOTEL ÖSTERREICHISCHER HOF
Manager: Elfi Kammerhofer
Schwarzstrasse 5–7
5020 Salzburg, Austria
Tel: (0662) 88.977 Fax: (0662) 88.977.14
120 Rooms, Double: AS 2,600–5,900
Open all year
Credit cards: all major
Restaurants open daily
USA Rep: LHW 800-223-6800
Across pedestrian bridge from Old City

The Schloss Mönchstein has an engaging façade—a jumble of towers, turrets, and crenelated roof lines, softened by clinging ivy that drapes the entire castle in a garland of green. Approaching the hotel along the private drive, you pass many fancy cars which correctly hint at the type of guest the Schloss Mönchstein attracts—a wealthy, sophisticated, glamorous clientele who enjoy its luxury and discreet privacy. The hotel is set in a large park, surrounded by meticulously groomed lawns and masses of brilliant flowers in well tended gardens. As you enter the hotel, a door to the left leads to a small chapel (frequently used for weddings). The lobby, lounges, and bedrooms are decorated in a sedate, formal manner, with many antiques, crystal chandeliers, Oriental rugs, and brocaded fabrics adding to the refined ambiance. The award-winning dining room is especially outstanding. With only 17 guestrooms, the hotel seems more like a private home than a hotel, and indeed it used to be the residence of the owners, the family von Mierka. Schloss Mönchstein is located in Salzburg on the Mönchsberg hill above the city. Although the tranquillity of the forest setting of the hotel makes Salzburg seem like a different world, it is only about a five-minute walk along a quiet forest path to the elevator that drops down the hill and lets you off in the heart of Salzburg.

HOTEL SCHLOSS MÖNCHSTEIN
Owners: Family von Mierka
Mönchsberg Park 26
5020 Salzburg, Austria
Tel: (0662) 84.85.550 Fax: (0662) 84.85.59
17 Rooms, Double: AS 2,400–22,000
Open all year
Credit cards: AX, MC
Restaurant open daily
USA Rep: Relais & Chateaux 212-856-0115
Located on hill overlooking Salzburg

Because Salzburg is such a popular tourist destination, most hotel rooms here are very expensive. One outstanding exception is the Hotel Wolf. Although making no pretense to be deluxe, it offers spotlessly clean rooms and the warmth of caring management. The hotel is conveniently located just off the Mozartplatz: this is a pedestrian zone, but you can drive your car in to drop off your luggage before parking. Glass front doors lead into a hallway with a couple of nondescript chairs and a sofa. Beyond is a reception desk where you will frequently find the gracious owner, Frau Rottensteiner. The 500-year-old house has been in her family since 1900 when her grandmother ran the hotel. Just off the entry hall is an arched-ceilinged breakfast room with white walls and Oriental carpets on the floor. At one end of the breakfast room is an attractive small sitting area with a handsome armoire and antique chest. The guestrooms are all located on the upper floors. Each of the bedrooms varies in decor, although they all have a similar ambiance, with fresh white walls, colorful rag rugs on wooden floors, and often a painted armoire. My favorite, 38, is a spacious room with blue-print draperies repeated in the same fabric on the headboard, painted armoire, light-pine side tables and chairs, and desk. Although the bedroom is spacious, the bathroom is very small. Room 27 has a much larger bathroom, but the decor is not quite as light and pretty. But no matter what room you are in, this is a real winner in Salzburg for hospitality and value.

HOTEL WOLF
Owners: Family Rottensteiner
Kaigasse 7
5020 Salzburg, Austria
Tel: (0662) 84.34.530 Fax: (0662) 84.24.234
15 Rooms, Double: AS 980–1,490
Open all year
Credit cards: AX
No restaurant: breakfast only
Middle of Old Salzburg

The Romantik Hotel Gmachl has been in the Gmachl family since 1583—Friedrich Gmachl, the present owner, is the 21st generation. The building is full of character: it was constructed in 1593 as a tavern for the Benedictine monks of the Monastery of Nonnberg, so it is even older than the beautiful small onion-domed church to the right of the hotel which also belongs to the Gmachl family. (Step next door to see the exquisite church and its graveyard where generations of the family are buried.) There have always been a farm and a butchery connected to the property and the tradition lives on with a family-owned, picture-perfect, small sausage shop on the left side of the hotel. The exterior of the hotel is most inviting: a soft, mustard-yellow façade with white-painted trim, flowerboxes at the windows, and a steeply pitched roof. Inside, a mood of elegant yet rustic charm prevails. There is a series of inviting lounges and intimate dining rooms. Family portraits, photographs, and memorabilia are everywhere, along with fresh bouquets of flowers and fine antiques. Some of the guestrooms are in the main building, others in a lovely old house across the street. All the bedrooms are beautifully decorated with great flair. Tucked into the garden behind the house is a large swimming pool. The Hotel Gmachl is expensive, but less so than comparable hotels in Salzburg, and it makes a convenient base for exploring the city (only 15 minutes' bus ride away).

ROMANTIK HOTEL GMACHL
Owners: Theresia & Friedrich Gmachl
Dorfstrasse 14
5161 Elixhausen-Salzburg, Austria
Tel: (0662) 48.02.12 Fax: (0662) 48.02.12.72
50 Rooms, Double: AS 1,820–2,920
Open all year
Credit cards: all major
Restaurant open daily
USA Rep: Euro-Connection 800-645-3876
8 km N of Salzburg

The Gasthof Gersberg Alm is not in downtown Salzburg, but situated on the Gaisberg, the mountain overlooking the city. The hotel has a guest shuttle going back and forth to Salzburg (approximately 60 shillings per person each way), making this tranquil location a convenient choice for those who prefer to stay in the countryside. Although the origin of the hotel was an old farmhouse, what you see is mostly new construction. However, the hotel is built to harmonize with the past and its style has the typical Tyrolean feel. The ground level is of white stucco with shuttered windows, while the next two stories are made of wood and have balconies draped with geraniums. In front of the hotel a green lawn, dotted with mature shade trees, slopes gently downward. To the right of the hotel is an outdoor garden terrace—a favorite place for lunch on a warm day. To the left of the hotel, on a raised terrace, there is a swimming pool. Inside, the hotel has a rustic charm. The lobby has a welcoming ambiance with light-wood paneling on the walls and ceiling and Tyrolean-style floral paintings on the front desk. Just off the lobby are a cozy bar and lounge. Throughout the public rooms there is a motif of rustic elegance—lovely furnishings with a country look. The guestrooms are spacious and nicely furnished, but are more modern in decor. The staff seems exceedingly friendly and well trained, although there is more the air of a commercial hotel than a little inn.

ROMANTIK GASTHOF GERSBERG ALM
Owners: Families Kreibich & Myslik
Gersberg 37
5023 Salzburg, Austria
Tel: (0662) 64.12.57 Fax: (0662) 64.12.57.80
40 Rooms, Double: AS 1,850–2,900
Open all year (except 2 weeks in February)
Credit cards: all major
Restaurant open daily
USA Rep: Euro-Connection 800-645-3876
9 km E of Salzburg, on Gaisberg mountain

Schärding is a postcard-pretty little town, looking more like a painted backdrop for an operetta than a "real" town. A fountain graces the central square which is encircled with gaily painted, narrow buildings whose roof lines step up in a wonderful assortment of shapes and designs. The effect is one of gaiety and charm. Every exceptionally pretty spot needs a good hotel and luckily Schärding has the Forstingers Wirtshaus, located half a block from the square. The façade is very old and quite simple: it is a boxy green building with an arched doorway. Within you are greeted with warmth, both from the cozy decor and from the Forstinger family who own the hotel. If you are not staying the night, you might still want to stop for a meal in one of the series of dining rooms which stretch the length of the building. These are all attractive, one having an interesting collection of antique fishing gear (Schärding is famous for its fishing). The bedrooms are decorated in a variety of styles: some are quite modern in their decor; a couple have beautiful antique painted furniture. My favorites were the rooms with new light-pine furniture and traditional rustic-style four-poster beds.

ROMANTIK HOTEL FORSTINGERS WIRTSHAUS
Owners: Family Forstinger
Unterer Stadtplatz 3
4780 Schärding am Inn
Upper Austria, Austria
Tel: (07712) 23.020 Fax: (07712) 23.023
20 Rooms, Double: AS 1,275
Open all year
Credit cards: all major
Restaurant open daily
Near German border
103 km N of Salzburg

The Romantik Hotel Hirschen is a most attractive inn dating from 1757. Within is one of the most beautiful dining rooms in Austria—here you find French-blue curtains contrasted against mellow wood-paneled walls, low ceilings with intricate pine paneling, blue tablecloths harmonizing with the blue draperies, sheer curtains trimmed in handmade lace, fresh flowers on the tables, rustic wooden carved chairs, and an old ceramic stove in the corner. In addition to my favorite, the Romantik Hotel Hirschen has four other dining rooms, each displaying its own cozy ambiance. Doing the decor justice, the food is delicious. The Hotel Hirschen is efficiently and warmly managed by Franz Fetz whose family has owned the hotel for many generations. The emphasis of this inn is the gourmet kitchen, but Herr Fetz also provides accommodations. In recent years additional guestrooms were added in an annex reached down a path behind the hotel. These rooms are rather small and quite modern, lacking the charm of the original building. We recommend you request one of the antique-style rooms in the original section—these are more expensive but worth the difference in price.

ROMANTIK HOTEL HIRSCHEN
Owner: Franz Fetz
Hof 14
6867 Schwarzenberg
Vorarlberg, Austria
Tel: (05512) 29.44 Fax: (05512) 29.44.20
35 Rooms, Double: AS 1,230–2,250
Open all year
Credit cards: all major
Restaurant open July to September
USA Rep: Euro-Connection 800-645-3876
14 km E of Dornbirn

Hotel Descriptions

The Schloss Obermayerhofen is an elegantly furnished castle in splendid condition, but what you see today is a recent transformation. Following World War II, the castle was used as a British occupation headquarters, then later abandoned for 45 years until rescued by Harald Kottulinsky. The property had been in his family since 1777—in fact, a title of nobility was bestowed upon his ancestors because of their bravery in battles against the Turks. The castle sits on a gentle wooded hill outside the town of Sebersdorf, isolated from, yet conveniently close to the A2 which runs from Vienna to Graz. There is no austere, foreboding quality to this pretty, pastel-yellow castle—it is appealing from first glance. Once you are through the outer gates, the Schloss Obermayerhofen appears directly ahead of you with a whimsical, blue-faced clock accenting the steeply pitched roof. You pass through a deep arched entry into an inner courtyard onto which most of the guestrooms face. Also off the courtyard is a family chapel, a favorite place for wedding parties who reserve the entire castle for their celebration. The guestrooms are exquisitely furnished. If you splurge on one of the deluxe rooms, which are enormous and sumptuously furnished, you will truly feel like royalty. The lounges and various dining rooms continue with the same degree of quality, refinement, and tasteful decor. What makes the castle even more special is the personal attention of the Kottulinskys who welcome guests into their home.

ROMANTIK HOTEL SCHLOSS OBERMAYERHOFEN
Owners: Brigitte & Harald Kottulinsky
8272 Sebersdorf, Styria, Austria
Tel: (03333) 25.03 Fax: (03333) 25.03.50
20 Rooms, Double: AS 1,700–3,000
Closed January & February
Credit cards: AX, VS
Restaurant open daily in summer
105 km S of Vienna, 53 km NE of Graz

Steyr is an exceptionally charming old town whose central plaza is lined with rainbow-hued medieval houses, most of them tall and narrow with red-tiled roofs. Perfectly located, facing the main plaza in the heart of the old town, are two especially attractive three-story houses joined together with a series of suspended arches. For over 300 years each house had been a hotel—one called the Inn of the Three Allies and the other the Inn of the Three Roses. The Mader family cleverly joined the two buildings to form the Hotel Mader. The renovation has produced an excellent hotel with each bedroom having its own private bath and direct-dial telephone. Although the bedrooms are modern in decor, they are very attractive, with nice wooden furniture, built-in headboards, white walls, colorful print draperies, and crisp white curtains. There are two restaurants which, like the lobby and lounges, have some antique accents. One of the most appealing and unusual parts of the hotel is the inner courtyard, surrounded by arcaded walkways, where meals are served in the summer. The Hotel Mader has been in the same family for over 100 years and their warmth and hospitality add greatly to the charm of this colorful inn.

HOTEL MADER
Owners: Family Mader
Stadtplatz 36
4400 Steyr
Upper Austria, Austria
Tel: (07252) 53.358 Fax: (07252) 5335.06
59 Rooms, Double: AS 1,180–1,240
Open all year
Credit cards: all major
Restaurant closed Sundays
40 km S of Linz

Steyr is a delightful small walled medieval town with a picturesque central plaza of colorfully painted houses. One of our hotel recommendations, Hotel Mader, has a choice location overlooking this charming square. However, Steyr has another stellar site where the Enns and Steyr rivers meet, and the Romantik Hotel Minichmayr has a prime location at this junction. The hotel is built to take advantage of its excellent setting with a small terraced garden at the entrance where guests can look across the river to the colorful medieval houses lining the river and beyond to the twin steeples of St. Michael's church. Inside, some of the decor seems a bit dated, but there is an ongoing renovation program and what can't be faulted is the genuine warmth shown. The guestrooms overlooking the river (such as room 241) are especially nice and definitely worth the extra price—the rooms have a standard "hotel look," but the water view is captivating. All of the guestrooms have TVs, mini-bars, direct-dial telephones, and hairdryers. There are also a sauna, solarium, and bicycles which guests can borrow free of charge. The hotel has two restaurants stretching across the back of the hotel, both with windows overlooking the river, and a cozy, paneled stüble.

ROMANTIK HOTEL MINICHMAYR
Owners: Isabella & Ingo Viertler
Haratzmüllerstrasse 1-3
4400 Steyr
Upper Austria, Austria
Tel: (07252) 53.410 Fax: (07252) 48.20.255
50 Rooms, Double: AS 1,346–1,796
Closed first two weeks in January
Credit cards: all major
Restaurant closed Sundays
USA Rep: Euro-Connection 800-645-3876
40 km S of Linz

The Haus am See is truly a stunning newcomer to the hotel scene at the gorgeous Weissensee. The hotel (opened in May, 1994) belongs to the Berger family and was built on the site of an old house owned by Helfried Berger's family. The location is prime—a large piece of land stretching out to the water's edge (the only lakefront hotel along the Weissensee). The large chalet-style, light-pine building has two wings embracing a lush lawn where guests can relax on chaise lounges or stroll across the grass to go swimming or boating off the private pier. Inside there is an open, spacious, uncluttered look with light wood used throughout in furnishings and paneling. One room flows into the next—the space is not divided by walls, but rather by defined areas. As you come in there are the reception desk on the left and two cozy sitting areas on the right, each with slip-covered chairs grouped around a separate fireplace. Beyond the lobby is a bar and farther on a splendid circular dining room wrapped with windows which overlook the lake. There is no effort to create a "pretend" antique ambiance: instead, the flavor is definitely of the country style, but with a contemporary flair. Lovely young Sonja Berger did the interior design and it is exceptionally alluring, with beautiful, English-style fabrics used throughout. The guestrooms, most with a view of the lake, are large and pretty, with beautiful fabrics setting a color scheme of blues and yellows.

HAUS AM SEE
Owners: Sonja & Helfried Berger
Techendorf 73
9762 Weissensee, Carinthia, Austria
Tel: (04713) 22.220 Fax: (04713) 22.228
33 Rooms, Double: AS 1,820–2,120*
*Includes breakfast & dinner
Open winter & mid-May to mid-October
Credit cards: none accepted
Restaurant open daily
170 km S of Salzburg, 56 km E of Villach

The Hotel im Palais Schwarzenberg is expensive, but no more so than any super deluxe hotel and its ambiance is truly sensational. Although only about a ten-minute walk to the heart of Vienna, you feel you are in an exquisite private home in the country. Here you live like royalty in an opulent 17th-century palace surrounded by over 18 acres of gardens where paths lead past manicured flower beds, arches of beech trees, fountains, and statues. The mood is refined, with a small reception lobby, elegant, antique-filled waiting room, cheerful tea room, formal dining room, and a glass-enclosed dining terrace. The decor is consistently pleasing, with lavish antique furniture artfully displayed, accented by priceless original art. Adding to the beauty of all the rooms are large floral bouquets—arranged by a member of the staff whose sole duty is to keep the hotel filled with flowers. The most deluxe of the guestrooms overlook the gardens— these sumptuous rooms are individually decorated and furnished in antiques. My favorite, number 6, is a corner room with walls covered in deep-green fabric. The least expensive bedrooms (also lovely) are in the new wing overlooking the parking courtyard. If you thought this must be the residence of royalty, you are correct: the owner of the hotel, Prince Von Schwarzenberg, still lives in one wing of the palace.

HOTEL IM PALAIS SCHWARZENBERG
Manager: Gerhard Schwendner
Schwarzenberg-Platz 9
1030 Vienna, Austria
Tel: (1) 79.84.515 Fax: (1) 79.84.714
42 Rooms, Double: AS 3,500–6,040
Open all year
Credit cards: all major
USA Rep: Relais & Chateaux 212-856-0115
In park, 10-minute walk to city center

For a moderately-priced hotel in the heart of Vienna, the König von Ungarn is outstanding. The yellow, three-story building with rows of gabled windows on its steep roof is on a side street just a block from St. Stephen's Cathedral. The ecclesiastical dignitaries used it as a guesthouse and stables until the early 1800s when it became a hotel. The name "König von Ungarn" (King from Hungary) is most appropriate since Hungarian nobles regularly rented apartments here: today, many of the rooms are named for these guests. Another famous guest, Mozart, lived in the house for several years during which time he composed *Le Nozze di Figaro*. The ambiance of these romantic bygone days lives on in this small characterful hotel. There is an intimate, refined ambiance from the time you step in the door. Just beyond the reception area the room opens up into a glass-roofed inner courtyard with comfortable groupings of chairs and sofas plus small tables surrounded by bentwood chairs. At one end of the room there is a cozy wooden bar where guests may order coffee or a refreshing drink. One wall of the courtyard is a yellow house with shutters. Other walls are beautifully paneled, with a gallery on the second level framed by windows. There is an elegant small dining room with marble columns, arched ceiling accents, soft lighting, and crystal chandeliers. The guestrooms continue the same quiet, tasteful, traditional ambiance.

KÖNIG VON UNGARN
Manager: Christian Binder
Schulerstrasse 10
1010 Vienna, Austria
Tel: (01) 51.58.40 Fax: (01) 51.58.48
33 Rooms, Double: AS 2,200
Open all year
Credit cards: all major
Restaurant closed Saturdays
One block from St. Stephen's Cathedral

The location of the Hotel Römischer Kaiser could not be more perfect—only a few minutes' walk to the Opera and just off the splendid pedestrian shopping street, the Kärntner Strasse. Even though in the heart of old Vienna, the hotel faces a quiet street where no cars are allowed, thus avoiding some of the noise and confusion of the city. (If you arrive by car, there is a back entrance that you can drive to.) In front of the hotel is a small terrace set with tables and chairs where guests can relax after a day of shopping or sightseeing. Entering the hotel, you find a pleasant reception lobby decorated with a crystal chandelier, Oriental carpets, and fancy chairs. A tiny lounge is to your right and an intimate breakfast room to your left. Although the ambiance is somewhat formal, the staff is extremely friendly, without a hint of stiffness. The Jungreuthmayer family own the hotel and personally oversee every element of its operation. Their dedication to the highest standards of management ensures your stay will be a most pleasant one. The Römischer Kaiser is a delightful small hotel with only 24 bedrooms: some are quite elaborate with ornate gilt furniture; others are more modern in their decor. All are well kept and attractive. Buffet breakfast is the only meal served, but this is no problem as there are many excellent restaurants just steps away.

HOTEL RÖMISCHER KAISER
Owners: Family Jungreuthmayer
Annagasse 16
1010 Vienna, Austria
Tel: (1) 51.27.751 Fax: (1) 51.27.75.113
24 Rooms, Double: AS 2,150–2,950
Open all year
Credit cards: all major
No restaurant: breakfast only
USA Rep: Best Western 800-528-1234
In heart of Vienna

For opera buffs there is no hotel more ideally situated than the Hotel Sacher: it is located just across the street from the world-renowned Opera House. For shopping enthusiasts, the setting is also fabulous as the most famous shopping street in Vienna, the Karntner Strasse, is just steps away. Although the Hotel Sacher is larger than most hotels included in this guide, it is a gem that glows with the romance and history of old Vienna. Since 1876 the Sacher has been the favorite gathering place for royalty, artists, politicians, opera singers, actors, and the beautiful people of Vienna. Step into the small corridor off the lounge to enjoy some of the nostalgic photographs of the Hotel Sacher's more famous guests. But it is not only sentimentalism and location that make this hotel so special: all of the rooms exude an opulent, old-fashioned elegance rarely found in hotels today. It has fine carpets so deep you sink into them, handsome mahogany moldings, red brocade fabric on the walls, brass polished to perfection, and gorgeous crystal chandeliers. Especially romantic is the inner courtyard, roofed over with a stained-glass skylight. There are several restaurants—especially popular is the elegant coffee house which opens onto the street. Here you can enjoy some of Vienna's famous coffee accompanied by a piece of the original Sacher torte—a chocolate cake with apricot filling which is so incredibly delicious that it's known throughout the world.

HOTEL SACHER
Manager: Reiner Heilmann
Philharmonikerstrasse 4
1015 Vienna, Austria
Tel: (1) 51.45 Fax: (1) 51.45.78.10
116 Rooms, Double: AS 4,020–5,560
Open all year
Credit cards: all major
Restaurants open daily
USA Rep: LHW 800-223-6800
In heart of Vienna, opposite Opera House

We almost didn't go in to take a look at the Pensione Susanna. Though the location is superb—it's just steps from the Opera House and only a block from one of Vienna's most prestigious gems, the Hotel Sacher—from the outside the Pensione Susanna looks quite hopeless: a nondescript, rather ugly concrete building with some kind of tacky "sex shop" next door. But because trusted friends had so highly recommended this small hotel as the best reasonably priced place to stay in Vienna, we rang the bell for the door to be opened, ventured into the dreary corridor, and climbed up one flight of steps to the reception of this small pension. What a surprise! To the right is a small room with an Oriental carpet and a tiny reception desk—here guests are warmly welcomed and given personal attention. There is no public lounge, but guests may sit in the breakfast room which is very pretty in a typical Viennese style—windows with lace curtains, wallpaper in tones of cream, gold sconce light fixtures, and four round tables surrounded by fancy chairs upholstered in turquoise-colored silk fabric. On the walls are prettily framed pictures of elegantly uniformed men riding spirited horses. The bedrooms are all similar in style, with pastel wallpaper, frilly curtains, and oil paintings and nicely framed prints on the walls. All the rooms have private bathrooms and the most expensive even have a small kitchenette. The Pensione Susanna offers far more value and hospitality for budget accommodations than you would expect in such an expensive tourist center as Vienna.

PENSIONE SUSANNA
Owner/Manager: Rudolf Strafinger
Walfischgasse 4, 1010 Vienna, Austria
Tel: (01) 51.32.507 Fax: (01) 51.32.500
25 Rooms, Double: AS 1,000–1,228
Open all year
Credit cards: none accepted
No restaurant: breakfast only
In heart of Vienna, one block from Opera House

The Residenz Altstadt happily bears little resemblance to your run-of-the-mill hotel. It is imbued with a warmth of hospitality and home like atmosphere rarely found in a commercial establishment. This is not happenstance, but a planned, well-thought-out intent by Otto Wiesenthal to provide guests an extra measure of caring. Before opening his hotel in 1991, Herr Wiesenthal was in the computer business where experiences in impersonal hotels inspired him to create an "ideal" inn where guests are welcomed as friends. Located outside the Inner Ring, the hotel is a leisurely 15-minute walk to the heart of Vienna's sightseeing. On a quiet side street, the hotel's discreet entrance is marked by a red awning and flanked by two potted trees. A staircase leads up one level to the reception area. The gracious hostess who checks you in also serves as a concierge who gladly assists with sightseeing plans, dinner reservations, and tickets for events. On the same floor there is a cozy lounge with an open fireplace and, just beyond, an appealing breakfast room. The bedrooms are all attractive and decorated with good taste. Many of the furnishings have a Biedermeier flair with just a touch of art deco thrown in for accent. Ask for one of the top-of-the-line guestrooms—they cost only a little more and are extraordinarily large. My favorite (number 31) is an especially cheerful room with large casement windows providing a romantic view over a tiny square to the pretty little St. Ulrich church.

RESIDENZ ALTSTADT VIENNA
Owner: Otto Ernst Wiesenthal
Kirchengasse 41
1070 Vienna, Austria
Tel: (01) 52.63.39.90 Fax: (01) 52.34.901
25 Rooms, Double: AS 1,550–1,680
Open all year
Credit cards: all major
No restaurant: breakfast only
USA Rep: Utell International 800-448-8355
15-minute walk to city center

The Hotel Zur Wiener Staatsoper offers a delightfully old-fashioned atmosphere right in the heart of Vienna. The room rates here are amazingly low for a hotel with such charm and quality of accommodations. Whereas most inexpensive hotels are rather bland outside, the Zur Wiener Staatsoper's façade is exceptionally attractive, with baroque plaster design enhancing the front door above which jaunty flags of many nations wave in the breeze. A filigree wrought-iron door leads into the gilt and crystal lobby area where your host, Walter Ungersbock, extends a warm welcome. The hotel faces onto a pedestrian street, so quiet prevails in the high-ceilinged guestrooms. Delicate flower-print wallpapers, matching curtains, crystal chandeliers, and reproduction white furniture create a fresh, feminine feeling in the bedrooms, all of which have a private bathroom, television, and telephone. There is no restaurant at the Zur Wiener Staatsoper: only breakfast is served. The breakfast room is pretty and inviting, with rose-toned tapestry chairs and old prints on the walls. Take advantage of the marvelous location of the Zur Wiener Staatsoper and go on foot to visit the many nearby coffeehouses and tempting shops along the Kärtner Strasse.

HOTEL ZUR WIENER STAATSOPER
Owner: Walter Ungersbock
Krugerstrasse 11
1010 Vienna, Austria
Tel: (1) 51.31.274 Fax: (1) 51.31.27.415
22 Rooms, Double: AS 1,300–1,550
Open all year
Credit cards: all major
No restaurant: breakfast only
Mid-way between Opera House & cathedral
In heart of Vienna, near Kärtner Strasse

The Romantik Hotel Post is very old—records going back to the 16th century show it as a palace belonging to the Counts of Khevenhuller. It is not known exactly when it was converted into a hotel, but official documents indicate it has been an inn since at least the beginning of the 18th century. Since that time it has been host to many famous persons including the Empress Maria Theresa. As the name implies, the hotel was a postal station many years ago, and the restaurant reflects its history with a charming mail-coach motif, with fascinating antique prints of old mail coaches artfully arranged on the walls. There are several other cozy dining rooms, one with a hunting motif with trophies displayed on the walls. Behind the hotel is a small courtyard where meals are served when the weather is warm. The bedrooms vary considerably: the least expensive are somewhat small and dated in decor. It is worth the extra cost to splurge and request one of the better rooms, such as 225—a large corner room which is very attractive. Although it seemed on our last visit that the hotel could use some fresh paint inside and redecorating to bring it back to its former glory, the Romantik Hotel Post continues to provide the best accommodations in Villach, which is a charming, old-world city.

ROMANTIK HOTEL POST
Owner: Dr F. Kreibich
Hauptplatz 26
9500 Villach
Carinthia, Austria
Tel: (04242) 26.10.10 Fax: (04242) 26.10.14.20
68 Rooms, Double: AS 860–1,700
Open all year
Credit cards: all major
USA Rep: Euro-Connection 800-645-3876
38 km W of Klagenfurt

The Hotel Schöneben is truly the perfect example of an Austrian country inn, both inside and out. Perched on a grassy hillside amidst spectacular mountain scenery, it is made up of two white plaster chalets, accented by dark-wood balconies overflowing with bright geraniums. Inside, a rustic elegance pervades the inn, whose oldest part dates from 1604, and you find a Tyrolean treasure chest of antiques, warm wood paneling, beamed ceilings, and fresh flowers. Pretty Alpine print fabrics adorn the dining-room windows and carved wooden chairs and tables grace the warm tile floors. Dinner on the terrace or in the cozy dining rooms is a romantic treat. Throughout this small inn special touches such as fresh flowers, lace curtains, and framed prints add warmth and charm. Host Stefan Schneider offers a selection of either standard doubles or suites, all with private bath and phone. Most of the guestrooms and all the suites have either a balcony or a garden terrace, and all are decorated with carved pine furniture. Although the double rooms exude a cozy charm, our favorite accommodations are in the "Achental" suites. Each of these has a bedroom, separate sitting area, and a terrace from which you have a stunning view across the valley to majestic mountain peaks. A visit here is a memorable experience, as Stefan Schneider's great love of Austria is expressed in every detail of the Schöneben and it seems as if the German term *gemütlichkeit* were invented to describe it. We really can't rave enough about this tiny inn—it is truly a dream.

HOTEL SCHÖNEBEN
Owner: Stefan Schneider
5742 Wald im Pinzgau, Tyrol, Austria
Tel: (06565) 82.890 Fax: (06565) 84.19
21 Rooms, Double: AS 1,200–1,700*
*Includes breakfast & dinner
Closed November
Credit cards: none accepted
Restaurant open daily for guests
75 km SE of Innsbruck

The Raffelsbergerhof is an outstanding small hotel located just a short stroll from the River Danube in the heart of Austria's scenic Wachau wine district. Long ago the house was the property of the controller of the river traffic, which must have been a lucrative job since the Raffelsbergerhof is an especially beautiful, spacious home. The outside is extremely appealing, looking much more like a French manor house than an Austrian inn. An enormous grapevine is cleverly espaliered across the length of the building which consists of two 16th-century, mansard-roofed houses joined by a two-story galleried walkway punctuated with a series of arches. You enter through heavy wooden doors into an inner courtyard formed by the two sections. The staircase to the right leads to private living quarters and the staircase to the left leads up to the second floor where the hotel reception desk is located. The hotel is most appealing—antique chests, old sleds, wrought-iron light fixtures, and fresh flowers lend a romantic ambiance. The bedrooms are spacious, clean, and attractive, with modern furnishings. The gracious Anton family own and manage this delightful small inn which displays high standards of excellence and great taste throughout. As a bonus, the room rates are very reasonable for a hotel of such quality and charm.

RAFFELSBERGERHOF
Owner: Claudia Anton
3610 Weissenkirchen, Lower Austria, Austria
Tel: (02715) 22.01 Fax: (02715) 22.01.27
12 Rooms, Double: AS 900–1,200
Open May to November
Credit cards: MC
No restaurant: breakfast only
Near the dock for Danube ferry
96 km NW of Vienna

The Zum Grünen Baum is quite an unexpected surprise. You would never expect to find a hotel with so much character and sophisticated charm in such a tranquil, off-the-beaten-path location. However, although the village of Ysper is tiny and untouristy, it is conveniently located for exploring this enticing region—close to the vineyards along the Danube and also convenient for visiting the many castles, churches, and abbeys in the area. Perhaps this small hotel has such heart because it has been in Frau Rotter's family for 350 years—always as an inn with an adjacent farm. The Rotters seem to accept a responsibility from their astounding heritage that ties them to the land, and thus have taken great care to preserve the authentic character of the house. The renovations have been accomplished with sensitivity and all of the rooms have a charming simplicity. From the moment you step into the entry hall, you are surrounded by a cozy, rustic ambiance that is achieved by the use of country-style antiques. Some are family heirlooms, others Frau Rotter has collected over the years. In addition to the painted armoires, old clocks, dowry chests, spinning wheels, farm implements, antique glass, colorful plates, and cradles, the walls display many original Austrian paintings that have been collected by Herr Rotter. But it is not the furnishings that make a stay here so special—it is the wonderful hospitality of your hosts whose sincere warmth of welcome is as genuine as their historical inn.

ZUM GRÜNEN BAUM
Owners: Family Rotter
3683 Ysper, Lower Austria, Austria
Tel: (07415) 218 Fax: (07415) 21.849
35 Rooms, Double: AS 798–1,029
Open all year
Credit cards: none accepted
Restaurant open daily
105 km W of Vienna, 1 km W of Altenmarkte

Hotel Descriptions

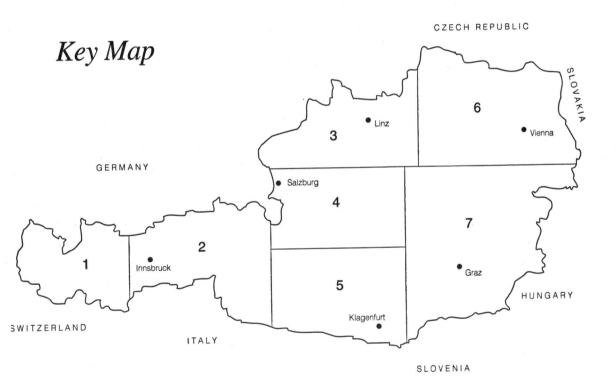

Key Map

CZECH REPUBLIC

SLOVAKIA

6

● Vienna

3

● Linz

GERMANY

● Salzburg

4

7

2

1

● Innsbruck

● Graz

5

HUNGARY

SWITZERLAND

● Klagenfurt

ITALY

SLOVENIA

191

Map 1

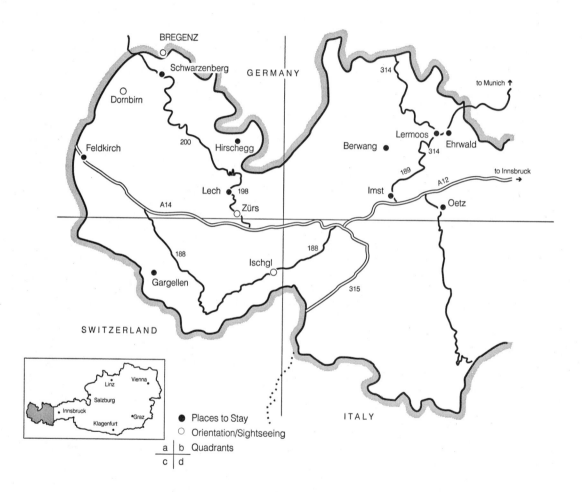

BREGENZ

Schwarzenberg

GERMANY

314

to Munich ↑

Dornbirn

Lermoos

Ehrwald

Feldkirch

200

Hirschegg

Berwang

314

Lech 198

189

to Innsbruck →

Zürs

A12

Imst

A14

Oetz

188

188

Ischgl

Gargellen

315

SWITZERLAND

Linz

Vienna

Salzburg

Innsbruck

Graz

Klagenfurt

● Places to Stay
○ Orientation/Sightseeing

a	b
c	d

Quadrants

ITALY

Map 2

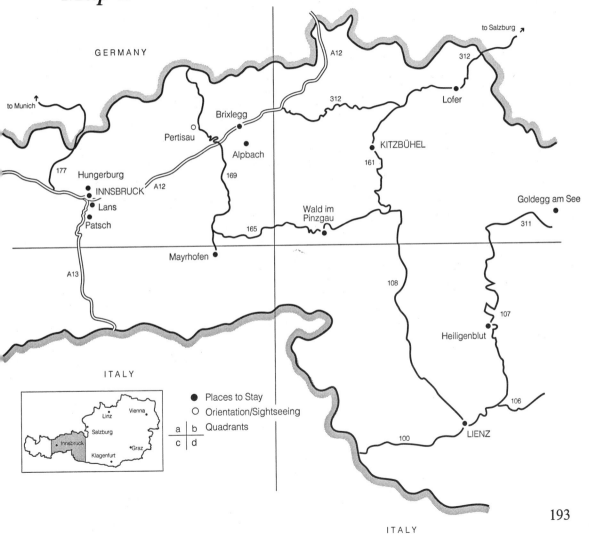

to Salzburg

GERMANY

to Munich

177

Hungerburg

INNSBRUCK

Lans

Patsch

A13

A12

Pertisau

Brixlegg

Alpbach

169

Mayrhofen

165

A12

312

312

Lofer

KITZBÜHEL

161

Wald im
Pinzgau

Goldegg am See

311

108

107

Heiligenblut

106

100

LIENZ

ITALY

ITALY

- ● Places to Stay
- ○ Orientation/Sightseeing

a	b	Quadrants
c	d	

Linz

Vienna

Salzburg

Innsbruck

•Graz

Klagenfurt

Map 3

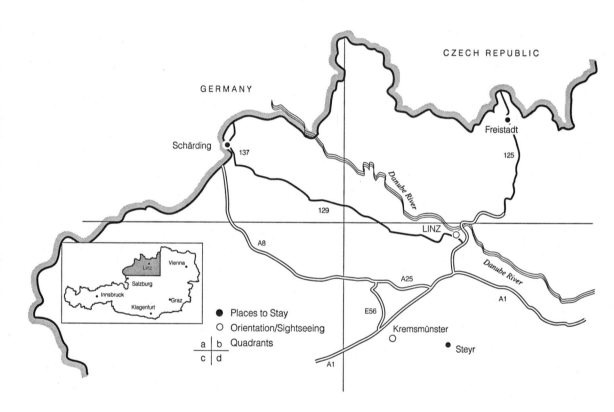

Map 4

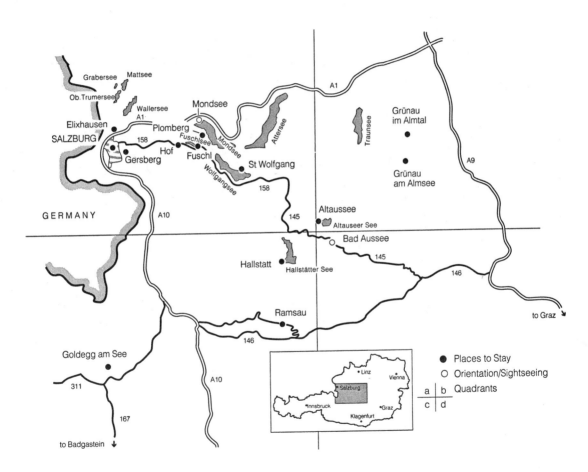

Grabersee Mattsee

Ob.Trumersee

Wallersee
A1

Elixhausen
SALZBURG

Plomberg
Fuschlsee

Hof
Gersberg   Fuschl

Mondsee

Mondsee

Attersee

St Wolfgang

Wolfgangsee

158

A1

158

GERMANY   A10

145

Altaussee

Altausseer See

Bad Aussee

Hallstatt

Hallstätter See

145

146

Traunsee

Grünau
im Almtal

Grünau
am Almsee

A9

to Graz

Ramsau

146

Goldegg am See

A10

311

167

to Badgastein

● Places to Stay
○ Orientation/Sightseeing

a	b
c	d

Quadrants

Linz   Vienna

Salzburg

Innsbruck   Graz

Klagenfurt

Map 5

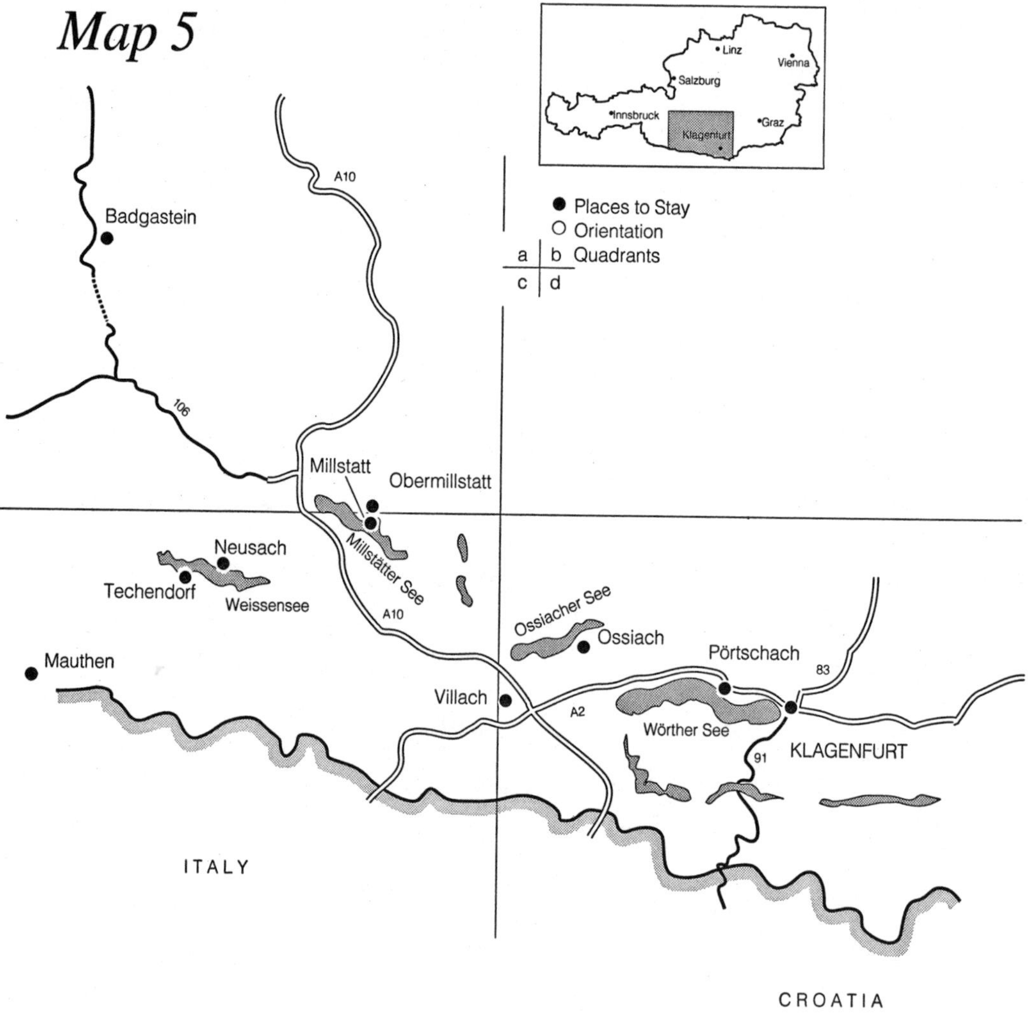

Linz
Vienna
Salzburg
Innsbruck
Graz
Klagenfurt
Places to Stay
Orientation
a
b
Quadrants
c
d
A10
Badgastein
106
Millstatt
Obermillstatt
Neusach
Techendorf
Weissensee
Millstätter See
A10
Ossiacher See
Ossiach
Pörtschach
83
Mauthen
Villach
A2
Wörther See
91
KLAGENFURT
ITALY
CROATIA

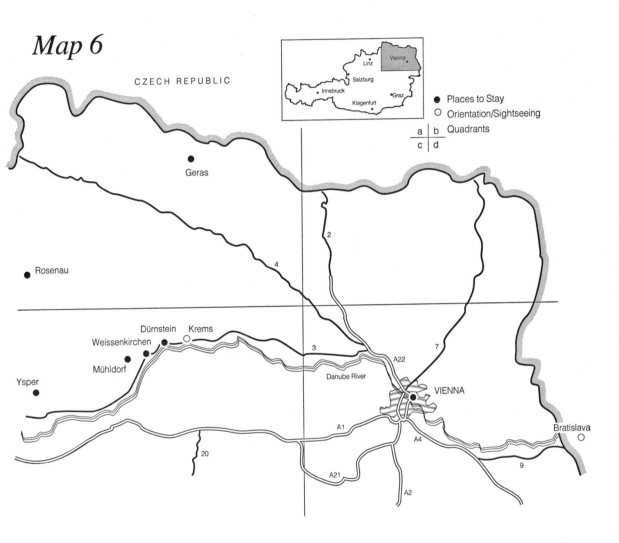

Map 6

CZECH REPUBLIC

Linz
Salzburg
Vienna
Innsbruck
Graz
Klagenfurt

● Places to Stay
○ Orientation/Sightseeing

a	b
c	d

Quadrants

● Geras

● Rosenau

2

4

Dürnstein   Krems ○

Weissenkirchen ●

● Mühldorf

3   7

Ysper ●   A22

Danube River

VIENNA ●

A1

Bratislava ○

A4

20

A21

9

A2

197

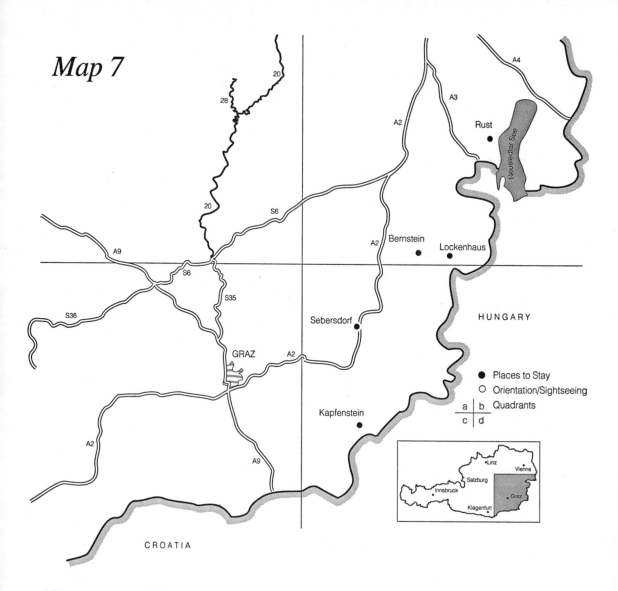

Map 7

20

28

20

S6

A9

S6

S35

S36

A2

GRAZ

A2

A2

A9

A2

Bernstein

Lockenhaus

A3

Rust

Neusiedler See

HUNGARY

Sebersdorf

Kapfenstein

● Places to Stay
○ Orientation/Sightseeing

a	b
c	d

Quadrants

CROATIA

A4

Linz

Vienna

Salzburg

Innsbruck

Graz

Klagenfurt

Index

Karen Brown presents

Karen Brown Travel Services
Providing all your travel needs

Book your air with us and our staff, trained by Karen Brown, is available to assist the individual traveler and the travel industry with:

- Special offerings on airline tickets and car rentals

- Personalized countryside mini-tours based on Karen Brown's Guides

- Reservations for hotels, inns and B&Bs in California and Europe, as featured in Karen Brown's Guides (subject to availability)

Quality, personal service, and great values

Call Karen Brown Travel Services today!
telephone: 1-800-782-2128
fax: 415-342-8292
e-mail: KBTRAVEL@aol.com
http://www.karenbrown.com

UNITED AIRLINES
is the preferred airline of Karen Brown's Guides and
Karen Brown Travel Services

Seal Cove Inn

Located in the San Francisco Bay Area

Karen Brown Herbert (best known as author of the Karen Brown's guides) and her husband, Rick, have put 20 years of experience into reality and opened their own superb hideaway, Seal Cove Inn. Spectacularly set amongst wild flowers and bordered by towering cypress trees, Seal Cove Inn looks out to the distant ocean over acres of county park: an oasis where you can enjoy secluded beaches, explore tidepools, watch frolicking seals, and follow the tree-lined path that traces the windswept ocean bluffs. Country antiques, original watercolors, flower-laden cradles, rich fabrics, and the gentle ticking of grandfather clocks create the perfect ambiance for a foggy day in front of the crackling log fire. Each bedroom is its own haven with a cozy sitting area before a wood-burning fireplace and doors opening onto a private balcony or patio with views to the park and ocean. Moss Beach is a 35-minute drive south of San Francisco, 6 miles north of the picturesque town of Half Moon Bay, and a few minutes from Princeton harbor with its colorful fishing boats and restaurants. Seal Cove Inn makes a perfect base for whale-watching, salmon-fishing excursions, day trips to San Francisco, exploring the coast, or, best of all, just a romantic interlude by the sea, time to relax and be pampered. Karen and Rick look forward to the pleasure of welcoming you to their coastal hideaway.

Seal Cove Inn, 221 Cypress Avenue, Moss Beach, California 94038, USA
Tel: (415) 728-7325   Fax: (415) 728-4116   E-mail: sealcove@coastside.net

Thank You For Your Kind Words

"When I came back from Italy last year I ordered all the Karen Brown guides to be sent to me in Hong Kong since they offer the best advice one can obtain from a guide book. We based our travels on your book and had the most wonderful time, thank you! We enjoyed our trip immensely and are busy planning our next trip around your guide." Melanie Pong, Hong Kong

"We used your guide "France: Charming Bed & Breakfasts" as our sole source of information on accommodations in the rural areas of the country. Your advice proved to be golden. Congratulations to you for your wisdom in selecting and describing these wonderful hosts." Betty and Bob Kelsey, Charlottesville, VA, USA

"My husband and I recently returned from a two week vacation touring the south and west of Ireland using your book as our guide. We had a marvelous trip, in large part, because your book is so accurate, easy to read, and well organized. Thanks for helping to make our vacation so terrific." Sandy Mullaney, Mashfield, MA, USA

*"I've been using your book for over five years now. I live in Italy with my Italian husband and we use your book **always** for our vacations, weekend getaways, and business trips. You guys have found everything! I'm always guaranteed a wonderful trip when I'm lucky enough to get a room in a hotel mentioned in your guide. Thanks for a great book and making living in Italy more enjoyable!"* Nancy Barker, Milan, Italy

"Thank you for creating your guide. I had vague stirrings toward the Dordogne/Lot, but hadn't a clue of where to go or what to do. Then, I found your guide—I'm sure you've heard this before, but it was exactly what I needed." Bruce Barnes, Mt. Shasta, CA, USA

"We like that we can trust you to have carefully scouted out and tested the places you recommend and your additional comments and notes on things to see are very useful. And all of this so logically organized and easy to reference! Thanks again for the good materials you keep providing and updating for all of us who need such expert guidance. With an new trip in mind, I always look for Karen Brown's input first." Denny Dudley, Iowa City, IA, USA

"Thank you, Karen, for your insightful and accurate recommendations. Our trip would not have had nearly the impact without these wonderful experiences." Holly and Gary Campbell, Atlanta, GA, USA

CLARE BROWN has many years of experience in the field of travel and has earned the designation of Certified Travel Consultant. Since 1969 she has specialized in planning itineraries to Europe using charming small hotels in the countryside for her clients. The focus of her job remains unchanged, but now her expertise is available to a larger audience—the readers of her daughter's country inn guides. Clare lives in Hillsborough, California, with her husband, Bill.

KAREN BROWN wrote her first travel guide in 1976. Her personalized travel series has grown to 12 titles and Karen and her small staff work diligently to keep all the guides updated. Karen, her husband, Rick, and their children, Alexandra and Richard, live on the coast south of San Francisco at their own country inn, Seal Cove Inn, in Moss Beach.

BARBARA TAPP, the talented artist who produces all of the hotel sketches and delightful illustrations in this guide, was raised in Australia where she studied in Sydney at the School of Interior Design. Although Barbara continues with freelance projects, she devotes much of her time to illustrating the Karen Brown guides. Barbara lives in Kensington, California, with her husband, Richard, their two sons, Jonothan and Alexander, and daughter, Georgia.

JANN POLLARD, the artist responsible for the beautiful painting on the cover of this guide, has studied art since childhood, and is well-known for her outstanding impressionistic-style watercolors which she has exhibited in numerous juried shows, winning many awards. Jann travels frequently to Europe (using Karen Brown's guides) where she loves to paint historical buildings. Jann lives in Burlingame, California, with her husband, Gene.

Order Form for 1997 Editions of Karen Brown's Guides

Please ask in your local bookstore for KAREN BROWN'S GUIDES. If the books you want are unavailable, you may order directly from the publisher. Books will be shipped immediately.

Austria: Charming Inns & Itineraries $17.95

California: Charming Inns & Itineraries $17.95

England: Charming Bed & Breakfasts $16.95

England, Wales & Scotland: Charming Hotels & Itineraries $17.95

France: Charming Bed & Breakfasts $16.95

France: Charming Inns & Itineraries $17.95

Germany: Charming Inns & Itineraries $17.95

Ireland: Charming Inns & Itineraries $17.95

Italy: Charming Bed & Breakfasts $16.95

Italy: Charming Inns & Itineraries $17.95

Spain: Charming Inns & Itineraries $17.95

Switzerland: Charming Inns & Itineraries $17.95

Name _____ Street _____

Town _____ State _____ Zip _____ Tel _____

Credit Card (MasterCard or Visa) _____ Exp _____

For additional information about Karen Brown's Guides visit our web site at karenbrown.com

For orders in the USA, add $4 for the first book and $1 for each additional book for shipment. California residents add 8.25% sales tax. Overseas orders add $10 per book for airmail shipment. Indicate number of copies of each title; fax or mail form with check or credit card information to:

KAREN BROWN'S GUIDES
Post Office Box 70, San Mateo, California 94401, USA
tel: (415) 342-9117   fax: (415) 342-9153   e-mail: karen@karenbrown.com